still gonna praise you

JAMIN ANNE HART

Still Gonna Praise You

Jamin Anne Hart

ISBN 978-1-7349323-0-0

Cover Design by Jeremy Hart for Hart Creative + Design

Published by Woodsong Publishing
Seymour, IN

Printed in United States of America.

Dedicated to

my parents, Joe and Anne Reece

and to my gift from God, Jeremy Hart

contents

introduction

How happy can a happy ending be if you do not walk the pages which tell it's story from beginning to end? The joy brought by a happy ending becomes cheap and under appreciated when pages are neglected and so much of the story is glossed over. To shortcut the journey is to lessen the impact of the journey's end. It is the story itself that really gives worth and reward.

On graduation day, it isn't flowers, cards, tassels, or the cap and gown that create a rewarding sense of accomplishment: it is the countless late nights and sleepless hours of diligent work and learning. Without them, the accomplishment would be empty and lacking. Isn't it the same in life? The moments that we despised living through are the very moments we look back on now with the understanding that they define who we are and who we are not. Those moments cause you to appreciate where we are now.

I must admit that when the opportunity of having a book published became possible, I felt inadequate in every way. It has been my dream from a very young age to write a book. Oh, how dear the memories are of those childhood trips to the library to scour the shelves, seeing what book titles caught my attention, loving the adrenaline rush of pulling undiscovered adventures off the shelf. I wasn't any happier than when diving into those new journeys with a hot drink in one hand, and those beautiful pages in the other. In fact, I did write many stories. I would run outside after dinner and sit on the hill in our backyard, smuggle some chocolate chips out of the kitchen cabinet, and get lost in thought as I wrote some dramatic, ridiculous and heart-wrenching novel. As I grew older, my aspirations grew also. They became something more. Gone was the dream of writing a timeless bestseller such as Pride And Prejudice or better yet, my beloved Anne of Green Gables. Yes, I still wanted to tell a story, but not just anybodies story or even somebody else's story. I wanted to tell my story. I wanted to write of my own pain and promise, gains and losses; to encourage another young lady—anyone—to keep living their lives for the One who writes upon our hearts and to remind us all how He truly does give us the desires of our hearts when we serve Him faithfully.

To see an author's book go around the world is an admirable accomplishment, but God has given me a contentment. If my story gets into the hand of one heart who will then draw closer to God, it will be reward enough for me. After all, it's all about His Kingdom and not one of my own.

Not long after getting married and beginning to write with the knowledge and intent of a book being published, I stopped. I felt embarrassed. My stories suddenly sounded cheesy when written on paper. They didn't hold enough intensity and dramatic action.

Humor was lacking. I didn't know where to begin or how to end. For a short time, I convinced myself I couldn't do it. For six months I didn't touch it. But in an altar one night, I felt the Lord renew my desire and speak to my heart, reminding me of the power of a testimony. If one person was impacted, it would be worth it all. So, I share my story not with arrogance nor shame; I share it with an overwhelming love for my Jesus and a confidence in Him. He is still our healer. He is still fulfilling the heartfelt desires of those who love him and are called according to his purpose. But you've still gotta praise him, even when the journey leads you to moments that you would love to skim over.

So, this is for you, dear reader. If you can find one story to relate to or hear the voice of God speak to your heart as you read, convicting and convincing you, that is all I desire. I have always learned and understood the most through personal stories. It is how I communicate; it is how I connect. It is how people identify with one another.

I have prayed many prayers over these words you are about to read. If you've felt, at times, that life won't get any better, this book is for you. The short truth is, it does, and when you stay faithful to God, He will bring you to tears of thankfulness. Truly, I am living in the fulfillment of my wildest dreams—and even beyond what I dared not to dream.

When I wrote the song, *Still Gonna Praise You,* in the quiet of a deserted class room at Indiana Bible College, I had no idea the people and places that it would reach. I can't explain how humbling and rewarding it is to hear a young mother, with emotion overflowing in her voice, tell me how *Still Gonna Praise You* got her through two long years of battling cancer. When she felt like she couldn't bear another day, she would close herself in her bedroom and sing this song until its message became the very sentiment of her heart. Whatever happened, she was determined to praise Him through it.

I nearly cried, myself, when a young girl came up to me and told me her parents' marriage had fallen apart. In her new home, away from the love that only parents can give, she listened to *Still Gonna Praise You* every day.

Countless times have I opened my social media apps and read messages from young ladies that I have never met, telling me of how this song became their anthem in the darkest moment of their life. Many of them faced unfathomable fear, depression and thoughts of suicide, but the song helped them to realize that their praise and devotion to the Lord could sustain their faith. Now, so many of those girls stand on the other side of their suffering with a testimony of God's faithfulness and a confidence in the power of their praise.

Hearing it sung by precious Filipino young people on the other side of the world, or recalling the moment my husband and I sang it at North American Youth Congress before twenty-five thousand people, is nothing short of surreal. The message is clear and gives no power to the enemy. In fact, on the contrary, the declaration of faith found in those lyrics have a profound way of defeating the adversary. Whatever attack or trial he may bring against us, the song proclaims that God is the one taking us through every low valley, and nothing will compromise our commitment to praise.

If this song has taught me anything, it is that our trials and triumphs have a far greater reaching effect than we ourselves could ever have. What you go through, and more importantly, how you go through it will determine the outcome. If our trust and confidence in the Lord remains steadfast, then nothing can be compared to the testimony that will be shared and the glory of God that will be revealed when the trial has passed.

I love what the Apostle Peter wrote in the first chapter and the seventh verse of his first epistle, "that the trial of your faith, being much more precious than of gold that perisheth, though it be tried with fire, might be found unto praise and honour and glory at the appearing of Jesus Christ." Any song that gets its listeners through a trial is, doubtless, a song born out of the author's own trials. I've certainly had trials, but I thank God for them. Every trial brought me to a triumphant place in Christ and now I say, in the words of the late Andre Crouch, "to God be the glory for the things He has done."

Looking back, however, it did not begin in that classroom when I put pen to paper and in a broken voice began to sing. The story began when I was a little girl in desperate need of a healing touch. Or perhaps the song was birthed out of the fear of losing my sister's life while she was being wheeled off to emergency surgery some seven hundred miles away. Those were the dire moments in which I whispered the words, even so Lord, I'm still gonna praise you. A song with any worth at all will burn as an anthem in your heart long before the words transfer from pen to paper.

This is my story. I share it with a confidence that my song is a song the angels cannot sing. This is the story of why I will forever sing, Lord, *I'm Still Gonna Praise You.*

CHAPTER ONE

a little

girl's dream

My life has never been void of adventures. I mean, have you ever wrapped a snowmobile around a tree? I can't say that it is among my proudest accomplishments of life, but that's just what happens when a wild middle child grows up with snowmobiles and four wheelers at her disposal.

It was Christmas day at Grandma Reece's farm. More than forty relatives made her big house seem small. Every kind of Christmas cookie was inside, and outside snowmobiles of every size, color and kind decorated the white lawn. They never sat idle for long. My dad and uncles organized a forty mile afternoon ride through the trails, leaving my cousins and myself to the cookies inside. I love cookies, especially the Christmas ones with sprinkles, but what I love even more is to be in the big middle of action and adventure. There wasn't much of that around the cookie tray, just moping faces and disheartened holiday cheer because of our being left behind. I looked out the window. There sat my dad's brand new Polaris snowmobile in the front yard. "He must've taken an older sled on the ride and left this one here," I told myself. It seemed like the answer to prayer! I just had to take it out for a run. My cousin Kaylin and I bundled up to beat the Minnesota weather and off we went, flying through the snow! Oh, how I love snowmobiling. We circled back around to Grandma's house and saw another cousin out in the yard taking pictures of the beautiful snow covered frozen lake, just down the hill from the house. Of course, I couldn't leave anyone out so I invited my cousin Rebekah to join the fun and jump on the snowmobile! "Isn't it made for only one passenger?" she nervously asked. I assured her with a confidence that I would later regret, "Oh, we can make it work!" So, all three of us piled on my dads new, shiny red Polaris snowmobile and off we flew over the hills and through the woods, seeing the snow covered pines as just a blur.

As I drove, Rebekah pulled out her camera again and began recording our ride. Something came over me. I just had to show off a little bit for the camera! Suddenly, my speed began to increase though those curving trails. I'm sure you could hear our giggles of pure joy on the far side of the lake. Speaking of the lake, our trail topped a hill and there at the bottom was a giant tree and the icy edge of the lake. With that deceptive over-confidence, I assured myself that if I raced down the hill and made a sharp turn at the right time, we'd clear the lake and tree and continue down the trail. Of course, my confidence didn't bother reminding me that the extra two passengers would make the snowmobile much harder to turn. Nevertheless, with lights, camera and action, I smashed the throttle and let gravity squish us up together on that seat as we darted down the hill. This is where my plan went wrong. The snowmobile would not turn, and before I knew it, POW! We slammed into the big tree!

Cousins went flying in every direction. The camera took up

wings as well—still videoing every moment, mind you. I somehow stayed on the machine, whose handlebars had bent backwards and pinned me down. I was too stunned to cry. I managed to maneuver out from under the grip of the handlebars and began checking to see if my cousins were still alive. Looking back over one shoulder and then the other, I saw them. They were alive, very much alive in fact. There they lay, sprawled out in the squishy snow, laughing.

I couldn't dare laugh, I was far too focused on the hood of this snowmobile being embedded into the tree. All feeling had escaped me, except panic. "Guys! We have to pull this snowmobile out of the tree before my dad sees!" As if we could dash up the hill, park it in the yard and he never notice the damage. Wiping snow off of our puffy outfits, we grunted and pulled with all our strength without a budge. The consequences were hitting me—dad's new snowmobile is in this tree and we can't get it out. How do I explain this? Well, lucky for me, I didn't have to—the video camera could explain it all.

We tried until we knew there was no use. I looked up to see my cousin Andrew on a snowmobile across the lake in front of us. Yes! Maybe he could help us! We waved him over and he, laughing, said we would have to wait for the uncles. I was sick to my stomach. The snowmobile had come to a smashing end, and I began to wonder if this would be my end, also. Not a moment passed before we heard the roar of a pack of Ski-Doo and Polaris snowmobiles coming across the frozen lake in front of us. The uncles had finished their ride and spotted us. Engines, one by one, were turned off, and then I heard the dreaded question, "What happened?" I can't even tell you what I muttered for a weak response. Within seconds, somehow those uncles and my father had it free from the tree. Thankfully, to my surprise, the engine still ran like a champ. My dad looked at me and said, "Jamin, you ride this one back with me."

The whole way up to the house I sat devastated. I was embarrassed. I felt helpless to pay for the damage. Hot tears leaked out of my eyes and froze onto my freezing helmet. When we parked in front of the shop, I could hardly look up. "Honey, what were you doing?" my dad asked. He never once yelled at us, but he had that lecture tone in his voice, and it broke my heart. He stopped though, mid sentence, and with kindness so undeserved, he looked at me and said, "Well, I'm just glad no one was hurt." Many more things could have been said and blame properly placed, but that was the end of the conversation. Oh, how I didn't deserve that kindness. My sincere apologies were met with unconditional love—endless, boundless, snowmobile-less love. If that doesn't show the incredible nature of my father, I don't know what will.

It is easy to love our heavenly father when you have an earthly father who shows such unconditional love. For those whose fathers were abusive and utterly unloving, I see clearly why they struggle to understand and receive the rich, pure love of God. I never doubted the love of God. At the center of His identify, our heavenly father is good and wants the very best for His children. No matter where you come from, let me remind you that our heavenly Father is good.

THE BEGINNING OF MY DREAMS

When the action, adventure and rides were all over, I equally loved being in the peaceful atmosphere of our living room, playing away at the piano and singing my little heart out. My love for music was always encouraged. When I wrote my first song at the age of six—a song that in full had two lines—my mom said she could just hear it being sung by a choir, and she truly meant it. I loved every opportunity I was given to sing with my mom and sister. Occasionally, we would visit other churches where my dad would preach and visit camps he had gone to growing up. No matter where we were, it seemed that just before service my dad would disappear for a few minutes and then show back up with a beaming grin, as if he was about to bust at his seams, informing us girls that they wanted us to sing a special. There was never a doubt in my mind about where he'd disappeared to and who had set that up.

The older I became, the more songs I wrote. Being a pastor's daughter, often we were invited into people's homes for dinner or to teach a Bible study. I loved those nights. If my dad had spotted a piano anywhere in their home, you could count on him causally mentioning that his daughter had a testimony and a song that she'd written. Minutes later there I would be, perched on a piano bench in someone's home, telling them about what Jesus had done for me and singing with all of my heart. Moments like that gave me purpose in life. I learned that a song from the heart, with a testimony behind it, could bring people to realize the realness of God. I was encouraged and gratified by knowing that they felt His presence. If the peace, hope, and love of Jesus was felt in their home for perhaps the first time, I was never happier.

To me, the highest compliment and ultimate purpose for music is to bring glory to God and to usher in His presence. In fact, the famous and accomplished composer Johannas Sebastian Bach said,

A Little Girl's Dream

"The aim and final end of all music should be none other than the Glory of God and the refreshment of the soul."

My favorite part of being a pastor's kid was having evangelists and missionaries in our home. On several occasions, the evangelist would park his family's RV in our driveway for the week of revival. I often would watch the evangelist's wife during the services, wishing I could be her and wondering what it was like to travel in an RV and minister in different churches all of the time. I wondered if she wore the same set of outfits from revival to revival, because who would know the difference? Every evangelist who came to our church had such happy marriages. When he called his wife to come to the piano to sing and testify, I always felt flooded with ambition and desire. I wanted that more than anything. Now, I see that it was far more than just sheer ambition and a childhood dream, it was something God was putting deep in my heart, a calling, whether I knew it at the time or not. Yet, like any good story, perfect days give way to unpredicted dilemma's that we fear will shatter our dreams. For us Christians, we often blame these devastating days on the enemy. Satan would love to destroy every dream that would lead us into our calling yet, be it the enemy or not, God allows and even uses those days when the dreams seems distant and fading.

As strange as it might seem, the enemy isn't always to blame. Sometimes the devil has nothing to do with our tough days. Sometime it is the expressed desire of God seeking to draw us closer to Him, the answer to prayers that we have prayed — "God, anoint me. God, use me. Let me have a testimony so people feel your presence when I minister."

Oh, what a prayer. Perhaps, if you have prayed this prayer then you have found, as I have, that God does not just pass out anointing like candy in a parade. Before the oil can flow over us, there must be sacrifice made within us. Trust and dependence upon God must be forged through the heat of trial and hardship. How else can we truly know Him? I have asked to see His glory. I have asked for His anointing. I have seen God answer those prayers, but not always how I assumed he would. Sometimes God answers our prayers by leading us down an adventurous road that we never would have chosen to walk, an adventure far greater than wrapping a snowmobile around a tree!

CHAPTER TWO

my

healer

No one prepares you for the moment the doctor looks at you and tells you to give up the very thing dearest to your heart. For this fifteen year old, it was singing. I don't pretend to be the greatest singer, because it was never about that for me. I sang as worship unto the Lord. It was my praise. Even more, it was my God-given calling. Singing had been put in my heart at such a young age to sing for the glory of God. I had seen the power of God's presence open up the hearts of congregations and minister to their soul as a humble heart sang under the anointing. I had been in services where the manifested presence of God left me in tears as I was moved by His glory. And if God could use me, that was all I desired.

I first noticed the pain while I was leading worship. How ironic, right? It was a Sunday morning at my home church and my jaw began to ache. I went home and casually mentioned it to my parents. We prayed in faith but, to an extent, shrugged it off, assuming that it was my wisdom teeth coming in and the pain would only be temporary. As any good precautionary mother would do, she scheduled a doctor's appointment for me so that x-rays could be taken. This would explain everything and did it ever explain more than I ever hoped to hear. As we sat awaiting the results, it never crossed my mind to be nervous. He would surely confirm our suspected theory of my wisdom teeth's arrival. Needless to say, I was shocked when the doctor came in and told me I had extreme temporomandibular joint disorder, commonly called TMJ. He said there was no cartilage on the left side of my jaw, and the other side had little left. I was speechless. He proceeded to tell me I could not chew gum anymore, which I did daily, but more importantly I could not sing anymore. Singing would put the most stress on it. He was only hopeful, at this point, of maintaining the damage and managing the pain. How unbelievable! I almost laughed when he said I could not sing anymore. I told him that was my world, I sang all the time! He weakly smiled and reiterated his previous statement. The extremity of the situation began dawning on me; this was really happening. The car ride home was made up of my mom encouraging me. I refused to shed one tear. It was confused denial. When I got home, I immediately ran to the piano and sang at the top of my lungs, banging the keys as hard as I could. To what end? I hoped in vein that I could show everyone—or myself, rather—that it was not true. Reality soon set in and seemed to say that I would not be able to sing my way out of this one. The aching returned. All through dinner my family encouraged me, but when I finished eating I locked myself in my dad's office and listened to my favorite song over and over and over again. It was the Avalon song, *Everything to Me*. Oh, how my heart identified with the line that said, "I want to live for Jesus so that someone else might see that He is everything to me." That was my one desire. No longer than that line was sung, the tears that I had earlier refused to shed came like a raging river.

How could this be? God had miraculously healed me as a baby and now called me to sing for Him. All I desired was to do His will and serve Him with my talents so that someone else might feel him the way I do, love him the way I love Him. It could have been something else: a broken arm, a ripped muscle, a torn rotator cuff, anything. But this, it wasn't fair. Singing was the very thing dearest to my heart. I reminded God of that very fact in that quiet moment. I know He heard me but knew that this was for my good. How else would I develop a deeper trust in God than to trust Him with what I held nearest and dearest? It had to be the thing closest to my heart for this story, my future, to have worth.

I googled "singers with TMJ" that night, which I now admit was neither my brightest nor most clever idea. Nevertheless, I read the names and stories of countless singers whose TMJ diagnosis brought their singing careers to a screeching halt. So much for the encouragement offered to me from my family! I was now sick to my stomach. Still not accepting it, I went to bed and, in prayer, reminded the Lord again that he had called me to sing; as if God needed a reminder.

Jaw pain and even TMJ itself seem like a silly thing to complain about until one has experienced how extreme and consuming the pain can be. For someone created to sing, it's like a death-sentence. Without this one sure confidence, can I be anything else? Can I do anything else? What does life mean now? It was my passion; my ministry!

Over the following months we went to a total of five different doctors and each one said the same thing: Do not sing anymore. It was destroying my jaw. In exchange for singing, I went to physical therapy three days a week and saw a chiropractor once a week, yet the pain worsened. It consumed my days, making it a heavy weight on the forefront of my mind. Before long my jaw no longer lined up, which made eating very difficult. There was clicking, locking, popping and pulling anytime I tried opening my mouth. Eventually it got to where I could hardly open my mouth at all. I was doing every exercise given to me by the therapist, but I saw no progress or healing.

Oh, how I cried. I cried when sitting on the front row in church trying to sing songs of worship, yet at the same time fighting the intense pain of a this life-altering condition. Even still, it was my worship, and pain should never silence our praise. On the contrary, it should give context to our praise. I cried in confusion. This wasn't some selfish prideful dream of being a singer that I possessed, I knew God had called me. When my bedroom door closed and I was alone, the moments were filled with frustration and prayer. Somewhere amid these quiet moments between God and myself, I discovered a dimension of faith that I hadn't known. After all, Paul wrote in Romans 12:3 "God hath dealt to every man the measure of faith." With overflowing love for my Savior, I proclaimed from the deepest part of my heart "even if God doesn't heal me, it will never change the way I serve Him." My praise would not be defined or determined by my pain and circumstances. I would still praise Him! So I continued on. I sang for Jesus at church, refusing to hold back my praise. Mondays would be the worst of mornings as I would wake up to find it hurting more intensely than it had the night before. The symptoms screamed in the face of my faith, "Where is your God now?" I knew God was with me. Perhaps that faith was unknowingly rooted in the remembrance of miracles that God had already done in my life. Even in my crib I had been healed.

When I was born, the doctors informed my parents that I had a teratoma tumor on my tailbone. On top of this, they said I also had spina bifida. Consequentially, they needed to remove part of my tailbone to get rid of the tumor. The doctor then made it clear to my parents that if I lived, and it was a big if, I would be handicapped, at best, and bound to a wheelchair for the rest of my life. A simple fall or sudden impact to the area of the tumor, could've left me instantly paralyzed. My mother was alone in the doctor's office that day when the news was given to her. That evening as she sat in our living room waiting for my dad to walk in from work, she really didn't know how to tell him, but somehow did. Without any hesitation, he hurried to the shelf above the kitchen sink and reached for the small bottle of anointing oil kept there. With that oil, he anointed my little body and prayed in faith believing and calling on the Name of Jesus for a miracle.

A section of my tailbone was later removed and, to everyone's surprise and delight, I took my first steps at eight months old. It was as if God was assuring my parents that their baby would be all right and His hand was upon her life. Years later, here I am. This wild, golden strawberry blonde who loves walking, running, hiking and riding on anything with speed and excitement now chooses to live her life, at its fullest, with thankfulness because life was given to her by divine order. Although every baby is a miracle, God made the miraculous my personal story. I have never questioned the existence of a God ordained plan for my life. When I consider the healing that God performed in my infancy, I am stirred to believe that His power will continually be revealed throughout my life. If he healed me before, He could heal me again.

Deep down, even with the unknown, I did trust God. I knew that God never calls us where the grace of God can not keep us. Despite moments of frustration, I now look back and remember the peace I had during this season. Isn't it comforting to know that we can walk through chaotic and confusing days but with the peace of God? With His peace, we can make it.

God's timing is so different than ours, yet always perfect. Eight long painful months went by. It was October and my dad had scheduled a weekend revival at our church with an evangelist. During the Friday night service, the evangelist prayed for my healing and deliverance from TMJ. It was powerful, but nothing seemed to change. The revival continued and on Sunday night, the last service of the weekend, my dad asked me to lead worship from the keyboard. I knew it would hurt, but I agreed. Eight months of pain hadn't changed my mind, I was still gonna praise Him.

During that worship service, a friend from my high school was visiting and came up to the altar. I will never forget my view from the key-board. I watched her respond to the presence of the Lord, raising her hands in surrender with tears streaming down her face. And while I sang through my pain, she was filled with the gift of the Holy Ghost. That is still the most beautiful sight of all: seeing people experience Jesus and, for the first time, receive His Spirit.

I sat down after the worship service overflowing with excitement for my friend. Then it hit me, my jaw didn't hurt! How could it be? "Is this really happening" I thought. It usually ached with intense pain for the rest of the evening, but not tonight. I was shocked, so much so that I did not tell anyone after church. Just in case the pain did kick in later, I would be the only one let down. Isn't that funny? We believe God is going to heal us, but we hardly believe it when the miracle actually happens!

When I woke up Monday morning it felt perfect. No pain! I jumped out of bed and ran to the mirror. Sure enough, I could completely open my mouth wide without any popping or clicking. My whole jaw lined up straight when I clenched down. I couldn't believe it! Actually, I did believe it and had to tell somebody! I raced down the stairs where I found both of me parents in the kitchen. My dad was about to walk out the door for work and I exploded with the news, full of rejoicing and hugs. I had once again been healed!

Oh, how perfect the ways and works of God are. Strange, frustrating, painful and long but, in the end, perfect. I suddenly saw it all so clearly. Just because the doctors were limited in their ability didn't at all mean that God was. It was the unfolding of a plan, and God often sends us to the point of extremity so that He can get all the glory! And oh how He deserves all glory, honor and praise.

Over and over, God has prompted me to reflect upon this miracle. I never cease to be amazed. It was amazing then and, to this day, I stand in awe of the amazing power of a miracle working God who is above, before and in the big middle of everything I face.

Not only did God heal me and enable me to once again pursuit His calling upon my life to sing, but something else also transpired that night. He called me yet again. Not only to sing, but I felt God call me to be an evangelist wife. I felt it so strongly that I wrote it down in my "God Journal" but, with the passing of time and living of life, I quite honestly forgot all about it. It wasn't until I started dating my husband almost eight years later that I found my journal again and was reminded of what I had felt and written down. Although I already knew it was God's perfect will for me to be with Jeremy, finding that paper was a beautiful confirmation of our being in the perfect will of the Lord. God was bringing my dreams, calling and desires full circle into fulfillment. Now, every time I stand on a platform with my husband and have the opportunity to testify and sing, I am reminded that He truly does work "all things together for our good, for those that love Him and are the called according to His purpose" (Romans 8:28).

A SONG WAS BORN

Mere months after being healed of TMJ, I was having devotion time with the Lord at the piano. No one was home, and I sat there in front of those keys just worshiping and talking to the Lord. It was such an ordinary scene, yet extraordinary as soon as God filled the room. Under the inspiration of God's Spirit, a song was born. There in my living room I sang it unto He who had miraculously healed my body so many times. I wanted to share it and let others know that He still heals today! Before getting up from that bench, I promised God that I would always share my testimony of healing every time I sang that song. Later, my mind began to dream of recording that song and sharing it with the world. Of course, I well knew who I was, just a blue eyed girl from small town Moose Lake, Minnesota. At the same time, I also knew my heart, and my heart longed to see people come to the knowledge of God's healing power. "So," I thought, "Who knows what might happen."

Over the three year period of time between the night I was

healed and my move to college, I was blessed with many opportunities to sing the song in various services and churches throughout Minnesota. During this time, one of my friends heard the song and came to know my whole story. Time passed and, while in my first year at Indiana Bible College, she texted me. "Jamin! I have TMJ, but I know God will heal me because he healed you, and yours was much worse." I instantly believed with her for a miracle of her own. That night she went to her church and, with complete faith, asked her pastor to pray for her. As God did for me, He did for her. She was miraculously healed that night!

Some time later, I was preparing to speak at my church. While writing down some notes on faith and healing, I heard the voice of the Lord speak to my heart. The Lord said, "I did not just heal you for you. I healed you for your friend and many more who will hear your testimony." Wow. It humbled me. It reminded me that while this did happen to me, it wasn't about me. Perhaps this healing, itself, wasn't even for my good as much as it was for the good of so many more that would receive their healing. I've come to believe with confidence that the Lord is not longing to heal alone but rather to give us a testimony of healing that we can share and use time and time again to bring glory to His Name. And so I took my testimony and shared it everywhere I had the chance.

Eight years after writing it, I was blessed to see God fulfill my dream of recording that song in a Nashville recording studio, with my husband. Our producer told me, "Sing it as if you just wrote it." With my hands raised in worship, I did just that.

Revelation 12:11 says of the saints of God, "they overcame him by the blood of the Lamb, and by the word of their testimony."

My Healer

When you have overcome something, you have authority over it. My husband and I have seen many healings in our travels because of this testimony and song. No, it is not because of me at all. It is all about Him Who is still our Healer. I have come to truly believe that He so desperately wants to heal His people, but they must allow Him too. So often we do not. Sometimes, it's because we don't ask. Sometimes, it's because we don't want it. Sometimes, it's because the change will be too great. But then there are other times when we pray for healing and hear the Lord say, "My grace is sufficient for thee."

Maybe we don't realize it, but we are seeing the same miracles performed today that were recorded in the book of Acts. I have watched sanctuaries become altars of healing from the power of one testimony. A man with pain in his leg that consumed his every day: gone. A women ready to commit suicide that night but instead was drawn to walk into a service in a country church, found Jesus in the altar, and walked out with a new hope and no thoughts of suicide. A young girl who had voices all around spewing words of how worthless she was, yet I danced with her in an altar as God filled her with His Spirit, speaking life and worth into the deepest part of her soul! How changed these moments leave us, and others! Speak it in boldness and in faith that God will use it to build up the faith of someone else. He is not only my healer, but He is your healer also.

CHAPTER THREE

falling in love

Perhaps the three most powerful words a human could utter or put on paper with a pen—I love you. In the way of young romance, there is nothing like hearing those words sincerely told to you for the first time. Jeremy first whispered those words to me in the pouring rain of a cloudy Indianapolis afternoon next to the Canals. I was speechless and unable to reply for a good 15 seconds, though it seemed like an eternity. Not only did I hear those sincere words, I saw the reflection of them in his eyes. I trusted Him. I wanted to memorize the moment of how he communicated the deepest feelings of his heart. A real security was formed in our relationship right there in the pouring rain. The three words he whispered were powerful, but there was character that stood behind them. Undeniably, I knew he was my forever.

I encourage you to read every Scripture in the Bible that pertains to love. Culture screams to us that love is lust, and that abuse is norm, but in the Word of God we find love so beautifully depicted and rightfully defined. In a world of distorted love, how comforting it is to see God's divine intention for perfect love. In simple definition, "God is love" (1 John 4:8); therefore, we must turn to Christ to see it in its purest form. When someone says he loves you, yet he portrays things opposing to Christ-like character, it is not true love. The truest of love is expressed only by the overflow of God's love in one's life. I have always said that I love who I am when I am close to Jesus. I feel better. I am happy. I am confident when drawn near to Him.

The claim of a Christian is a claim to love the Lord. I cannot write this book without talking about what it means to truly love the Lord. For if my words have any reaching affect at all, I refuse to let anyone be cheated out of the deepest relationship we could ever know. In fact, in all reality, my written words could never reach as far as God's own Word; therefore, I won't attempt to interpret or summarize the meaning of love and relationship. Let us look directly at the Word of God. It clearly states in Deuteronomy 6:4 that loving the Lord must be done with all our heart, soul, mind and strength. When this was declared to Israel, they knew without question that their love wasn't to be segmented, separated or expressed half-heartedly. Every part of them, their every fiber, was required. Every thought, action, behavior and area of their life was to be subjected to their love for God.

> *Know therefore that the Lord thy God, he is God, the faithful God, which keepeth covenant and mercy with them that love him and keep his commandments to a thousand generations.*
> *Deuteronomy 7:9*

God's sure way of identifying their love for Him was in observing their obedience to keep His commandments. "If ye love me," Jesus said, "keep my commandments" (John 14:15).

And hereby we do know that we know him, if we keep his command-
ments. He that saith, I know him, and keepeth not his command-
ments, is a liar, and the truth is not in him. But whoso keepeth his
word, in him verily is the love of God perfected: hereby know we
that we are in him. He that saith he abideth in him ought himself
also so to walk, even as he walked. Brethren, I write no new com-
mandment unto you, but an old commandment which ye had from
the beginning. The old commandment is the word which ye have
heard from the beginning.
1 John 2:3-7

Do not love the world or the things in the world. If anyone loves
the world, the love of the Father is not in him. For all that is in the
world, the lust of the flesh, and the lust of the eyes, and the pride
of life, is not of the Father, but is of the world. And the world
passeth away, and the lust thereof: but he that doeth the will of
God abideth for ever.
1 John 2:15-17

When reading these descriptions of love in Scripture, one cannot help but be convicted and convinced. No, it is not man's words;
they are God's infallible, living words. They are not dead or dor-
mant words of a dead relic of days gone by. They are the eternal
Words of a living God. In fact, God is His Word.

In the beginning was the Word, and the Word was with God, and
the Word was God.
John 1:1

So, this living Word requires, of our own living, that we love Him and keep His commandments.

FAKE CHRISTIANS IN A REAL WORLD

It isn't fair to God or man for this world to see Christianity so misrepresented. In the book of Isaiah, God expressed the heaviness of His heart because of the people of Israel. Remember, these were the people of Judah carrying His Name, yet worshiping idols and participating in all things worldly and full of lust. Their hearts were far from the one they claimed to serve. Even their sacrifices were a mockery to the Lord, ritualistic routines just to numb the slightest sense of conviction.

The world isn't foolish. When we claim to be Christian and hold dear the name of Jesus, yet serve the same idols they do, it cheapens their perception of God. The world is left utterly uninterested in turning toward a God whose own people are far from Him. If they are to see Jesus, it must be through a people who are an authentic, Biblical reflection of Him. Can the world see Jesus through you? I have come to realize that however perfect or even pitiful one may look on the outside, without Jesus in their lives they can do nothing but desperately search for something real, not some temporary experience that leaves them unchanged and absent of a difference, but a real encounter and relationship with God.

Jesus used trees and fruit as a metaphor of our lives and influence when He said, "Every good tree bringeth forth good fruit; but a corrupt tree bringeth forth evil fruit" (Matthew 7:17). We all, whether we be born again Christians or rebelling sinners, are known by our fruit. "Even a child is known by his doings, whether his work be pure, and whether it be right" (Proverbs 20:11). If a person is truly full of the Spirit of God, then you will know them by the fruits of the Spirit, which can only sprout from a heart rooted deep in God.

But the fruit of the Spirit is love, joy, peace, forbearance, kindness, goodness, faithfulness, gentleness and self-control. Against such things there is no law.
Galatians 5:22-23

In the quiet moments of a late night devotion, I came to a convicting understanding. We love the first three fruits. Although society certainly struggles to accept the truth of what real love, joy and peace are, they are not unfamiliar concepts. We commonly see those words knitted on pillows, printed on T-shirts and painted on canvas, but when's the last time you saw patience (forbearance) being celebrated? Faithfulness? Gentleness? Or how about self-control? How come those words are not knitted into the fabric of our homes and set out as reminders of who we are to be as children of God? I was convicted, yet again. To truly be filled with His Spirit, there must be fruits of not only love, joy and peace, but also patience, kindness, goodness, faithfulness, gentleness and self-control. We find one fruit that is easiest to couple with our natural personality traits and consider ourselves a saint, never endeavoring to grow in the Spirit and produce the other good fruit as well. Maybe our homes and lives need to be filled with more reminders of that which we should be striving to attain. That is why we must continually read the Word of God. We can't be convicted by something that we haven't surrounded ourselves with. As that revelation dawned upon me that evening, I prayed that God would give me more of the fruit I lacked. Lord, give me more patience. The very next morning, we had to be at the airport at six o'clock in the morning for a flight. I was asked to stand an extra hour in a long airport security line just because my TSA pre-check didn't work. Once I got through, would you believe that the coffee shop was out of the exact item on the menu that I so desperately wanted! I had to laugh. God really does take our prayers seriously. Patience was what I had prayed for the night before and, against my own convenience, I had already been given every opportunity to grow that fruit. God never just hands out fruit, but rather He gives us opportunities to discipline ourselves into developing and incorporating them into our character.

Now, thinking on those Scriptures, they make sense, don't they? They require work and diligence on our part but are not, at all, an impossible challenge. God has not asked or expected too much of us; therefore, we must respond with actions of obedience. To show our love to any husband, mother, sister or father, we must obey and listen to their words. Hearing, listening and reading isn't sufficient when there has been a call to action. The common cliché says that actions speak louder than words, and I think we could all agree that words are cheap when there has been no action behind them.

Even God surely feels cheated when we profess to love Him by cheap words but mock Him by careless actions. Oh, how His heart must break when those who claim to know him so blatantly defy His Word and forsake His commandments. Every law and commandment in the Bible is written out of pure goodness and love for us as protection from sin and its consequences. When we rebel against those principles and truths, we cannot escape heartbreak, disaster and even evil itself.

Let's talk about it. Why purity? Why does the Bible speak so plainly about sexual purity? This is counter-culture. Are God's guidelines still relevant in this post-modern world? By looking around at times, it may seem that commitment has become an un-familiar vow, but it is undoubtedly still reverenced and revered by those who seek to please the Lord in all that they do. The lasting pain of failure is even greater than any measure of temporary plea-sure. Regardless of the circumstance, a fleeting moment of pleasure will not negate the wounds and life-long scars that one's confidence, character and self-esteem will bear for the rest of one's life. Outside the beautiful boundaries of a Christ-centered marriage, the phys-ical act of forsaking purity is nearly impossible for a girl to move beyond without real pain, deep hurt and regret. Of course, those results are not promoted or warned of in today's secular agenda, but Scripture gives clear understanding of sin and its consequence.

For the wages of sin is death; but the gift of God is eternal life through Jesus Christ our Lord.
Romans 6:23

So, I choose to live within the safety of His Word.

In my senior year of high school I had a friend who openly pro-claimed to be Christian and held fast to the Scripture that says, "All things work together for the good" (Romans 8:28). She often quot-ed it to me when desperately trying to justify her sin of partying, sleeping around and disobeying the Word of God. The problem with false justification of sin is that it is never thorough or valid. Justification always has more holes than a fish net. That very Scripture that she tried to use as her shield of protection was actually the same Scripture that, in its true context, should have pierced the conscience of her soul and pricked her heart.

All things work together for good to them that love him and are called according to his purpose.
Romans 8:28

Christ cannot work it out for our good if it is not aligned with and centered around His purpose, His Word or His Will. In all of His grace and love, He is also just and will never contradict His Word. Though not always ordained or approved, God may mercifully use things to bring about the fulfillment of His Word, but He will never overlook or neglect His Word for things. His Word will never be sacrificed; not for a man nor for the exalting of anything above Himself. He is truth and out of Him speaks no lie or contraction of what He has said. To seek justification of wrong with such charismatic deception only plunges one into deeper darkness. The working together of good is only brought to pass through the expelling of darkness by light. Where there is the light of truth and righteousness, and our desires have been turned toward things godly and pure, then will the goodness and mercy of God follow us.

Understanding the uncompromising nature of God, and even the standard of obedience and submission that He requires of us, gives us the ability and confidence to trust Him. We can enter into relationship and covenant with Him without reason to fear, confident that He will never fail or forsake us. What a privilege to truly trust in God, knowing undoubtedly that He is true and faithful. The real clincher concerning trust is not our trust in God but His trust in us. It must go both ways. How ridiculous of us to expect trustworthiness of Him, yet never live trustworthy ourselves. We get so self-centered and self-exalting that we hinge our surrender to God upon the evaluation of whether we consider Him worthy of our trust and confidence. "Can I trust Him with my heart?" we ask ourselves. In reality, that isn't the real question. What should really be asked of ourselves and considered in all sincerity is this question: "Can He trust me?"

Could you bring yourself to truly trust someone who talks a good talk but never listens to what you say or does what you ask of them? Not at all, so how could we expect God to operate any differently? We must completely align ourselves with His Word and earnestly endeavor to please Him in all that we say and do. Many Christians today believe and practice the Word of God only in part. They believe only what seems easy enough to integrate into their desired lifestyle and discard the rest as if it were written for or required only of some other time period and people. What the writer of Hebrews said of Jesus is also true of His Word: It is the same yesterday, today and forever. His Word is just as true today as it has ever been. It hasn't lost any power, authority, effectiveness or reliability. It is timeless, eternal and "...endureth to all generations" (Psalm 100:5). His Word is for us right now, today.

The words of Jesus, that many hate to be reminded of, are these: "Be ye holy, as I am holy" (1 Peter 1:16). That requires repentance and consecration, whereby we daily take up our crosses and follow Him. We must daily strive to attain likeness unto Him, to know Him in the beauty of holiness. I refuse to argue and debate about what we can do or cannot do and still make it to heaven. My one concern and all consuming question is this: How close can I be to Jesus? That is all that really matters. That is what will get me into heaven. The peace that comes with being close to Him is unmatchable. The joy I find there is unspeakable. The love shown toward me is perfect and boundless.

When that question ceases to be our concern, when our focus is on anything but our relationship with Him, without fail, our lives will become empty and full of misery. Though there may still be breathe in our lungs, it is not real life. Real life is in Jesus. Nothing compares to the incredible sense of peace, contentment and fullness found when getting up from a time of prayer on your knees. The satisfactory feeling of knowing that you were in the holy presence of the one true living God, knowing that you are His and He is yours, simply cannot be matched.

KNOWING HIM FOR MYSELF

My sisters and I were the youth group in our church growing up. We didn't have a youth pastor or a bus load of thirty kids, it was just us girls. It would've been easy to dwell on what we missed out on and the things we didn't have, but God allowed me to see the beauty of all that I did have. I had godly parents. I had a church. I had truth. I had Jesus. I didn't need a crowd of others my age all doing the same as I did to live for Him. I only needed Him. He alone was my motivation, not youth parties or game nights or some cute boy that just started coming to church. I fell in love with Jesus.

46

It doesn't matter if you are in a youth group of one or a hundred and one, the only thing that matters is your relationship with Jesus. Find your security and confidence, not in a crowd or in the affirmation of a booming student ministry, but in the God that knows you and loves you.

I cannot express to you how much value, meaning and happiness was added to my life by moments of daily prayer in my bedroom. I would walk around my bed and just talk to God, telling Him everything. Eventually, after many tears and tissues, I'd end up opening my Bible and find a Scripture that spoke to me. In true preachers-kid fashion, I would then stand up on the bench in my room and pretend to preach that thought to the largest of audiences. I know playing church is just what kids do, but I really wasn't playing. It was more to me than just a game or a pass-time. Sure, when we were younger it was especially fun when the sisters came to my services and revival broke out among our Barbie dolls, but it wasn't just fun and games. There was a desire rooted deep in our hearts to experience the power of God. Furthermore, I wanted others to know and to feel Him like I had felt Him and come to know Him. I wanted other girls and boys to know that even if you are the only one in the Sunday morning youth class, that's okay. Loving and truly knowing Jesus is all that really matters.

When I became old enough to drive, like any sixteen year old, I wanted to go somewhere because sitting at home was no longer necessary. I would jump in my Impala LS and, in the middle of the day, go to the church, not for a service, revival or get-together. I would go alone and, for hours, play the piano and sing for an audience of one. I didn't need anyone to hear me; it was for Jesus. So often, my song would be brought to a halting stop as the presence of God became so strong that I couldn't carry on. I would leave the piano and fall down in the altar with tears streaming down my face, earnestly and humbly moved by the unbelievable realization that God would love me enough to respond to my praise.

Those moments gave me such confidence and strength. I undoubtedly, by experience, knew God and had felt His glory. I knew not only who He was, but who I was in Him. It gave me so much joy. I knew that I walked in divine favor with God. Wherever I went and whatever I faced, I was certain that God was always right there with me. That is the true beauty and benefit of following God's will for our lives; we are able to then live in His abundant blessings and walk in the safety and protection of His power. Where His Word leads, it will also keep. Where His Will carries, it will comfort. As much as His commandments govern, they also guard. I pray that we never lose our love for God and passion to pursue His presence.

TIME WITH HIM CHANGES EVERYTHING

Someone once told me of a broken and bitter man. He had been bitterly hurt by religion and people quite unlike Christ. Hurt had led him to give up. This man was done. On Sunday morning, he confidently approached the pastor and emphatically informed him that he would never set his foot inside the church again. He was mad: at people, at the pastor, at religion, even at God. The pastor nodded and said he understood, but asked one thing before leaving for good, "Step into the prayer room for a few minutes and let God know that you're leaving and why." The man carelessly agreed, seeing as it was his last time in the church anyways, and stepped into the prayer room and began talking to God. Pacing back and forth, he told God how mad he was and explained every bitter reason of why he wouldn't be back to His house. As the words rolled off of His lips, petty sounding in the light of the prayer room, something happened. God's presence flooded that room in response to a hurting man who was on the brink of bowing out on God. Though his words that day were harsh and accusing, far from loving, they were also honest and sincere. God always responds to the honesty of our hearts. As God's presence drew near unto Him, the man stopped pacing. Words now seemed unnecessary. With His Glory all around, in brokenness the man whispered, "but God, you are still good and I do still love you. I remember when you saved me. You did what nothing or no one else could ever do." The tears that then flowed from his eyes could've floated the ark as he fell to his knees in complete surrender. God always responds to brokenness. Psalms 51:17 reminds us, "the sacrifices of God are a broken spirit. A broken and contrite heart, O God, thou wilt not despise." God couldn't ignore the honesty and brokenness of this man, and met with Him powerfully. What a reminder to us once again, we should never shy away from His presence when we are broken or even upset. On the contrary, it is in those moments God cannot despise us: He will meet with us.

Later, when the man opened the prayer room door again and walked out to approach the pastor, in a broken trembling voice said "I'll see you next Sunday morning." He never stopped coming.

There are no other words needed to explain what happens when we take our trouble to God in prayer and cast our every care upon Him. The Scripture is true, "... he careth for you" (1 Peter

5:7). In His presence we find burdens are lifted, hurts are healed, wounds are mended, worries are vanished and loving arms are wrapped around us. As the song was so adequately penned by Jonathan Butler, "Falling in love with Jesus is still the best thing I've ever done."

CHAPTER FOUR

falling out of love

Jeremy and I had been married almost six months, six months of marital bliss. We were leading worship at a youth camp in Oklahoma that summer and gearing up for the exhaustive busyness that comes along with camp. The night before camp started, we decided to take advantage of a relaxing evening in the motorhome. Each of us sat comfortably engaged in our own activities, unwinding. For me it ended in a scroll though my social media. While perusing the happenings of all my friends, I came across an article that, being a newlywed, caught my attention: "How to Tell if Your Spouse is Falling Out of Love with You."

Deep down I knew I should probably keep scrolling and resist this streak of curious fear. Silly me, of course he still loved me! But I did it. I clicked. There on my own couch I sat spellbound by this article, wondering if it could be true. My mind was blown, and according to my husband, so was my logic.

The article said that one way to tell if he has fallen out of love is if he no longer waits for you. You know, when you get out of the car to go eat or shop, he shouldn't dash off and leave you in the dust. He should wait and walk beside you hand in hand! If he doesn't, you have a problem. The article said, he doesn't love you anymore.

As I read that, my mind began racing. I couldn't remember if he always stood and waited for me whenever we did our errands, so I made up my mind to put it to the test tomorrow. Shocking, I know.

The next morning, we made a quick stop at Walmart to pick up a few things for the week of camp. "Now remember," Jeremy said, "we have to hurry because we have a band rehearsal in 30 minutes. We can't be late." As we pulled into the parking space I decided now was the time to see if he still loved me. He jumped out and walked around to open my door. Now, looking back, that should've been proof enough against this articles diagnosis on our relationship, but no. I stepped out and as he closed the door, I stood there to see if he would wait for me. Right there, between a handicapped parking space and the always unorganized shopping basket receptacle, our relationship was over. I couldn't believe it! He was already around the corner of our car and three parking spaces toward the door while I stood there in hopeless despair. I kept waiting to see if he would come back for me and then he turned around. "Come on, we've got to hurry!" he said. I caught up but was utterly in awe of the confirmed fact that our marriage had fallen apart so quickly.

Once inside, I tested out the theory three more times. I intentionally lagged behind, appearing to look at something that I honestly cared nothing about. Every time he boogied right along down the aisle trying to find the things on our list. I caught up and, once, he even commented that I was moving slow that day. Of course, in dramatic fashion, I didn't respond. I was too worried about the bigger picture. Our marriage was struggling! Now, surely you see the humor in this and have come to the same conclusion I now have. I must have been delusional by exhaustion. My emotions were running wild and, apparently, I was riding the roller coaster for all it was worth. It sounds silly to you I'm sure, but it was real to me in that moment. I couldn't help but think of the future. Would there even be one now?

We turned to pass down the yarn aisle, and I couldn't take it anymore. I burst out loud with the question of the hour, "Do you even love me anymore?" Yes, I admit that wasn't my brightest moment and definitely wasn't the best thing to say to an incredibly loving and devoted husband. "Of course I do," he said. "What makes you think I don't?" The confused frustration in his voice was evident. He had every right to be frustrated, yet there I stood with tears pouring down my face. Amid the arts and crafts supplies, I told him everything. Oh, how I wish I could've tapped into the creative atmosphere of that aisle and spontaneously conjured up a good cop-out story to relieve the pressure of the moment and cover up my misplaced confidence in our relationship. Nope, I had no other choice but to spill the beans all down aisle seven. "I read this article on social media." Needless to say, the conversation ended with this emotional feeler promising to never read those ridiculous online media posts again. In case you were wondering, we barely made it to that practice on time. Thank God, because being late requires a good excuse, and this sure wasn't one.

CALLING LOVE INTO QUESTION

Isn't it amazing that I would question the love of the man who has never given me a reason to question his love toward me? It seems completely irrational and unreasonable, yet one ignorant article and my mistake of reading it made my mind overreact. Although this was something that happened between my husband and me, and we now laugh about, I later realized how we often treat God the same way. A sinless Savior who demonstrated His great love by laying down his life for us, suffering the excruciating pain of the cross and rising up out of the grave so that we can be raised up also, we often question. Something unfortunate happens in our life and we insult the Lord by wondering in ourselves, "Does God love me anymore? If He did, how could he let that happen to me?" Perhaps even more often we sin, repent, fall into the same sin again and find ourselves wondering if God still loves us after all of our failures. We feel as though we have messed up beyond our measure of grace and are forever unworthy for his love, as if we were ever worthy to begin with.

We are made worthy by God's grace, and by that grace we are saved. It is the very essence of why we were created. His love is grounded in one desire: to have a relationship with his creation. In return, knowing Him that formed us in the womb is what gives purpose, confidence and joy deep within us. Jesus is the only one who can fill the void which hungers within us to be filled. Only time in His presence can change us and, even, our situations. When we truly fall in love with Jesus and develop a close relationship with Him, we then discover the whole point of living.

That is exactly why the enemy of our soul so often whispers the lie that our sin has surpassed the place where the love of God can reach. Believing that lie, we pull away and are too ashamed to talk to God. We feel too dirty to be in His presence. If you have felt this way, be encouraged because you are not the only one. In fact, the first couple of the universe felt those same feelings. The influential appeal of the serpent brought about their choice to sin, which caused Adam and Eve to hide themselves from God. Up until their sin, they were blessed with the beautiful privilege of fellowshipping with God in the cool of the day. This time in God's presence was more beautiful than any tree, stream or waterfall that might've lavished their paradisal garden. What we sometimes fail to realize is that God saw their sin and still showed up for their daily appointment. When Adam & Eve didn't show up because of their shame, God asked His first question recorded in the Bible; "Adam, Where art thou?" It was not their sin that he questioned, it was their absence from His presence. So, for the first time, God questioned his creation. Of course, God knew exactly where they were, and He knew exactly what they had done. The reason for His asking was to show forth His unchanging love for mankind even after failure. Even still today, the heart of God must hurt when we pull away and hide from Him, yet still He calls out to us.

As humorous as the disastrous social media experience is, it does not dispute the truth that waiting is an expression of love. The definition of the word wait is to stay where one is until something happens.

I remember being ten years old at junior youth camp. There was a bell that rang, indicating that it was time to assemble for the next session. Instead of racing to the tabernacle, I lagged behind and continued watching the boy that I had developed a crush on that week. I waited in hope that he would come talk to me. As the other rowdy kids rushed to class, that boy walked over and waited for another girl, and together they walked across the campground.

She had to have felt like the most important person in the world, or at least the prettiest at camp, all because someone had stayed behind to wait on her. I know I would've felt that way, but instead I stood off in the distance feeling rejected and disheartened.

Perhaps God was asking Adam and Eve what I wanted to ask that boy, "Why aren't you waiting on me?" He wondered if they would still show up and spend time with Him again; would they be honest and open before Him? That is what captures the attention of heaven! Communication is what turns that heart of God. Although that was long before the blood of Christ was shed for our forgiveness at Calvary, we see a fore-shadowing of Jesus' sacrifice in the blood of the animal that was slain so that Adam and Eve could obtain a covering for their naked bodies. To be covered, there had to be blood shed. I thank God for the blood that was shed so that I could be covered and clothed in righteousness and holiness. Repentance makes that possible.

The question is never "Does God love me?" or "Will He wait on me?" God is always waiting on us. I believe God is the one who asks the question. It's the same question He asked Peter after he denied knowing Jesus three times: "do you love me?" God can't help but wonder, when we take off doing our own thing without any regard to Him and His will, do we wait on Him? Do we spend time with Him in prayer anymore? Do we set our phones down long enough to talk to Him in the quiet of our homes? Have we used entertainment and self-glory to cover ourselves or are we still dependent upon His grace to cover our sin? I believe God is saying, "Here I am, waiting for you."

We think we are waiting on God. We like to think that God is the one running late. It's God that isn't answering. It's God that has changed. Poor innocent us, always having to wait on God. In an effort to salvage our pride and save our righteous image, we want others to know that we are waiting on God's blessings to come into our lives. By faith, or so we call it, we are waiting on that promotion. "I'm waiting on the Lord and soon He'll give me every desire of my heart." But are we, really? I believe more than we are waiting on an answer from God, God is waiting on us to get ourselves out of the way long enough to seek Him for who He us. God waits on us to turn our waiting room into a prayer room. God help us to set aside our selfish way of thinking and our tendency to distract ourselves with entertainment until we forget our purpose.

LOVE AND ACTION

Throughout my teenage years, I spent time every day with God in devotion and prayer. It was my favorite time of day. It made me who I was and gave me confidence and joy. It gave purpose and context to every part of my life. With age comes both responsibility and distractions, which means we must be more intentional in our walk with God. If we do love Him, then we must intentionally show it in our actions. I made prayer my comfort zone. It became my safe place. When big, hard things came my way I knew I could always run to that place where I was most comfortable. I could always run to God in prayer. It's the same for you: you run to who you know will be there for you. I knew without a doubt that Jesus was Who I could count on to always be there when I needed Him.

Even within the realm of ministry, it can be easy to sacrifice our relationship with Him by doing so many things for Him. It breaks my heart and fills me with conviction to think of how many times God has asked the question of me: "Jamin, where art thou? Do you still love me? You haven't waited on me in a long time. You used to wait for me in my presence. You used to go to your bedroom every day and wait on me as you read my Word. You used to wait on me in worship, but now there are times that your mind is far from worship, only thinking of what the rest of the day entails."

Christ's message to the church in Revelation was this, "I know thy works, and thy labour, and thy patience, and how thou canst not bear them which are evil…Nevertheless I have somewhat against thee, because thou hast left thy first love" (Revelation 2:2,4). Wow! We can be faithful to the house of God, we can live in obedience to His Word, we can dwell in the protection and favor that comes from adhering to His commandments, we can hate ungodliness, yet what does it matter if we do not love Him like we first loved Him? If we forsake time with Jesus, what is the purpose of serving Him? Can we represent his Name, yet be absent from the relationship that we claim to have? There's no way! What a misrepresentation that is to the world around us.

In Luke 10, Jesus was at the house of those well known sisters of the Bible, Mary and Martha. Jesus was received of them and sat, perhaps, in the living room fully accessible. With great hunger and sensitivity to the Lord, Mary found her place at the feet of Jesus. How content she was to just hear His voice and be there in close proximity to the God who had changed her life. The Bible says that Martha was cumbered about much serving. While overcome with stress in the kitchen and frustrated beyond measure, she tattled on Mary to Jesus because her help was needed and there she sat at

His feet. After all, Martha was doing all of this for Him! Jesus answered in Luke 10:41-42 and said, "Martha, Martha, thou art careful and troubled about many things: But one thing is needful: and Mary hath chosen that good part, which shall not be taken away from her." Whatever your place of service might be, or someday be, in the kingdom of God, we must never get so caught up and consumed by our duty that we forsake our devotion and time spent at His feet. I am not at all saying that we should forsake our duties, nor can we forsake our devotion. There must be a disciplined balance in our lives of both duty and devotion that keep our priority and purpose in line with God's will.

In John 14:15 Jesus said, "if you love me, keep my commandments." That is as clear as it can possibly be. We cannot say we love him and not show it in our actions. Love requires action. We must obey His Word, follow His commandments and know Him in the power of His Spirit.

That I may know him, and the power of his resurrection, and the fellowship of his sufferings, being made conformable unto his death. Philippians 3:10

You do not know a friend until you've spend quality time with them. In fact, are they even really your friend until then? No, they are at best just an acquaintance. So it is with God. To know Him is to love Him and to love Him is to act as one who is loved by Him.

A WAITING SAVIOR

It was at a well in Samaria where Jesus stopped and waited on a woman. It was His love that led Him there and His love would keep Him there until her life was changed. Her sinful ways and ill reputation did not drive Him away or call forth a change in His mind. Jesus well knew what she had done and yet, when she arrived to draw water and began conversing with Him, He revealed himself unto her saying, "I am He." Lady, that is why I am here. I've been waiting to let you know that I am the Christ! It was that revelation that prompted her to lay her sinful life aside and whole-heartedly serve this God who had patiently waited for the moment when His love could intersect with her life.

This may be a new day and different era, but it has not changed. Lives are still changed at the well-side of God's ever-patient love. It is our open and honest conversation that God is waiting for. You may not understand the fullness of who He is or what He's up to, that woman of Samaria sure didn't, yet God can reveal and make clear His love only through a heart and mind that is open unto Him. Just talk with Him! Don't shut Him out and enjoy making God wait. Let yourself trust Him and be transformed by a moment at the well.

Isn't that all we want in a relationship? Time. Our time is precious and how we spend it goes to show what is most precious to us. Can there be anything more precious than time with the Almighty God? Those moments of fellowship are where we truly develop love for Him and trust in Him. God's desire in those moments is that we would come to understand who He is. Some would say that's a complex subject, but it's really quite simple. Who is He? He is goodness. He is mercy. He is grace. He is unlike any other. Satan so desperately endeavors to distract us from time spent in personal prayer and devotion with God because He well understands the power of relationship. Satan once had close relationship with God and now despises the thought of us having what he forever lost. I pray I never lose that. May I forever yearn for His presence, to sit together with Him in heavenly places, to hear His voice, to feel His touch. No, I don't at all desire to be above Him—there is no one higher—yet my simple and sincerest desire is to be as close to Him as I possibly can. Spend enough time with Him and you'll soon realize that you cannot live without Him.

Perhaps, the enemies greatest desire is to make us feel so worthless that we avoid the presence of God. He, of course, hopes that time spent away from Him will destroy any trace of relationship. He's absolutely right. Distance is the death that has taken so many lives to their spiritual graves, because outside of Jesus Christ there is no true life. Distance doesn't heal or soothe when it comes to knowing God, or any relationship, it only drives a wedge.

Satan says, "You are so unworthy" and the funny thing is, he's right about that one! I'm utterly unworthy, even on my best day! The prophet Isaiah said, "We are all as an unclean thing, and all our righteousnesses are as filthy rags" (Isaiah 64:6), yet we must never fail to remind Satan that Christ was "made...to be sin for us, who knew no sin; that we might be made the righteousness of God in him" (2 Corinthians 5:21). Though I be unworthy, His righteousness has made me worthy. How amazing His grace is. So amazing that "if we confess our sins, he is faithful and just to forgive us our sins, and to cleanse us from all unrighteousness" (1 John 1:9). For every time Satan tells you that you're unworthy, tell Satan how you became worthy. Every time he reminds you of your past, remind him of your testimony.

If you do not have a relationship with God wherein you obey His Word and walk in His commandments, spending time with Him every day, I pray I could convince you to develop just that. There is nothing like talking to the Lord about your day. Whether it be from behind your steering wheel in traffic, amid a crowded classroom of godlessness and blasphemy or in the quiet of your home. He responds with strength, peace and favor to the cry of those who come seeking Him.

Have you fallen out of love with your Savior? I pray you never do. Cling to His Word and hide it in your heart. Live a life filled with His Spirit. Love and long for His presence every day. Do the things that love requires. Do not let daily Bible reading become ritualistic and mundane. Don't just read the first Scripture you see someone post on social media and consider that to be your source of spiritual food. Pick up the Book and read a chapter. Read a few chapters! Let every line come alive. Let those words of eternal life speak to your heart, mind and soul. What I write to you, so did the Apostle Paul write to Timothy, "Study to shew thyself approved unto God...rightly dividing the word of truth" (2 Timothy 2:15).

And pray! Pray big prayers! Watch Him answer those big prayers and fall more in love with Him. Don't just send up a little "Thank you Jesus" here and a "Help me Lord" there. Relationship with God takes more than a seven second request for God to bless your day. In fact, what if God wanted to direct us in a certain way or warn us of a certain path? Do we stop long enough to allow Him to speak? Take some time and pray until you feel His presence. While there, tell Him about your deepest desires and watch them come alive. There's nothing any more exciting than seeing God change the life of someone you've been praying for or to watch Him intervene in a situation that you've been interceding for. That is the nature of God and the power of prayer. And while we all love answered prayers, I pray that we would fall in love all the more with prayer itself. There is no relationship where there is no communication. Prayer is where we find true fellowship with God. It's the one sure way to never fall out of love; a true love that gives you the confidence we all desire.

CHAPTER FIVE

beauty and
the beast

One thing have I desired of the LORD, that will I seek after; that I may dwell in the house of the LORD all the days of my life, to behold the beauty of the LORD, and to inquire in his temple.
Psalm 27:4

Give unto the LORD the glory due unto his name: bring an offering, and come before him: worship the LORD in the beauty of holiness.
1 Chronicles 16:29

Thine eyes shall see the king in his beauty: they shall behold the land that is very far off.
Isaiah 33:17

In that day shall the LORD of hosts be for a crown of glory, and for a diadem of beauty, unto the residue of his people.
Isaiah 28:5

Beauty and the Beast, or simply put, beauty and the ugly—those words depict such contrasting definitions. Have you ever felt like one or the other, or maybe both at times? I have! I remember feeling like the ugliest girl in the room. In fact, I felt that if I didn't lose twenty to thirty pounds and get a convincing tan that I could not be confident, much less beautiful. There was a season in which I desperately searched for beauty—at the mall, in the gym, at the salad bar. I lost twenty pounds and had darling new outfits but was empty inside. I was the emptiest I had ever been before. I had looked for visible fulfillment and validation on the outside, hoping that it would fill the empty longing on the inside. I felt as if God was so far away, yet now I look back at that season and see that He was perhaps the closest He had ever been. God is a Spirit and by the in-filling of His Spirit, we are made the temple of the Holy Ghost. Yet in this vulnerable season, I failed to understand the fullness of what that really meant for me as a young adult trying to find herself. In a season feeling conscious of my worth—feeling perhaps if I would have been more beautiful, friends wouldn't have walked away—I got caught up in looking at the outward and failed to look inward and be reminded of what I had. Often, inward is the very last place we look for fulfillment. Why do we always search outward?

THE ATTRACTIVE NATURE OF BEAUTY

Somehow every conversation pertaining to a man or a woman naturally gives a place for the question to be asked, "Are they beautiful? Are they cute? Are they attractive?" You've heard the dreaded reply, "They have a great personality!" Of course, that is not the compliment that it might at first sound like. No matter how much interest might have culminated up to that moment, it all vanishes as the conversation quickly takes an awkward turn to nowhere fast.

When I was engaged to Jeremy, I attended a high school performance of "Beauty and the Beast." I was with my mom and sister for one last hoorah before wedding chaos came upon us. The tale really is as old as time. As the amateur actors and actresses began reciting their lines, I couldn't help but look past the performance and close in on the content of the narrative: a beautiful girl wants a handsome man to love and cherish her. Perhaps because of my happily en-gaged state, I was more attentive to the dynamics of the love story being portrayed. It was his kindness that began to change and draw her heart toward him. I understood. Though it was a fictional storyline, I identified with those same overwhelmed feelings of loving kindness which were anything but fictional to my unfolding love story. Jeremy had shown to be the most kind person I had ever met. Even still, his kindness and gentleness cause me to continually fall more deeply in love every day. It's his character; who he is at his core. What stands above all else to me in that story is that as beastly as his outward appearance portrayed, who he was made her fall in love. When she saw what laid underneath the beastly persona of his appearance, he then became the most handsome man she had ever laid her eyes on.

Our hearts determine what we see as beautiful. What we love is considered beautiful to us and attracts us toward itself. Therefore it is so vitally important to daily spend time with Jesus, seeing first hand His character and kindness in our lives. The more time spent with Him, the more we fall in love with Him and are attracted to Him and His beauty; letting all else be defined, first and foremost, by the beauty of godliness in our lives. Without this we naturally see His Word as nothing more than some beastly rules that bind and restrict us from having what the world calls fun. Godliness becomes a barrier in our way while striving to attain a secular standard of glamor. But do we really know what beauty is or even who the beast is? Satan has done his absolute best to present a false pretense of disguise when, without doubt, he is the real beast; distorting and contorting our view and perception of true beauty. In the Bible, the word beauty is often synonymous with the glory of God. Therefore, with the Bible guiding us in all areas of our lives, what we consider beautiful should be the things which honor and bring glory to God.

DEFINING BEAUTY

If we lack understanding of true beauty then we form our opinion based on what we've been told beauty is. Billboards, social media, marketing, advertisements and magazines all propagate their ideas of what beauty is in our current society. To women in Asia, it calls for double eyelid surgery, which adds creases to their eyelids, to help them get a job or at least be happy when they look into the mirror. There is a fascinating online video containing the stories of beautiful Chinese women who have undergone plastic surgery. Joy said, "If I can get prettier, why not try?" She has spent over $90,000 and dozens of surgeries. One woman said, "I only had one thought; if the operation succeeded, great. If it failed and I didn't have money to fix it, then I'd kill myself." Another said, "If you wait, you've already wasted years of being ugly. If you're the only one not getting cosmetic surgery done, you'll be left behind." For this reason, about four million Chinese women have gone under the knife. One of these Chinese women said, "When you can't have something, you long for it and your desire never stops growing." Another lady said, "My face is worth $30,000. It is an investment. It is my happiness." There is no price too high that they will not gladly pay to attain more beauty.

What we lack becomes the benchmark of what we feel we should strive to attain. To women in the Philippines, beauty is depicted by white skin. They undergo skin whitening or bleaching procedures which are promoted on billboards with catch phrases such as, "whiter skin from within" or "fair and handsome." Even the Philippine national basketball team has an official skin whitening product. "There is a price for beauty," they say, "it is an investment." Along with it comes better jobs and, even perhaps, a better chance at love. Oh, how we all want that. Of course, there are side effects and skin damage disclaimers that accompany these procedures and products. In some countries, such as Ghana and Rwanda, skin whitening has been banned all together due to the high health risks. Nevertheless, the industry is making oodles of money, and people continue try to buy their beauty. An unaffordable price they will willingly pay just to have a better chance at attaining some unrealistic man-made idea.

In contrast to the Philippine standard, we Americans are told that being dark and tan is what equates beauty. Only reaching that standard are we told that we are stunning. It is the incessant pressure to be what you are not. So, let's entertain the question that Hollywood would never recognize for fear of jeopardizing their monopoly: why is beauty unattainable? Why it is so complicated and even unnatural? There is a price. There is a risk. So, we tan ourselves silly or, for those in other countries, buy unaffordable whitening creams for a chance at the beauty depicted by the media. They claim to be the experts and trend setters for what is beautiful. They shape our thinking and unfortunately we allow it, unless we have truth to combat it. The beast tells us beauty is sexual and buyable, so we shop. We spend untold fortunes, until we come to the marvelous understanding that it has been purchased in full! 1 Corinthians 6:20 tells us, "For ye are bought with a price: therefore glorify God in your body, and in your spirit, which are God's." Our one concern and goal should be that in all things we glorify God, for only in Him can one unveil the splendor of true beauty. If you have a price, the devil will pay it. If you have the understanding that you are priceless and already been bought with a price, the devil cannot buy you for anything, not a boyfriend, a dream career or brightly lit stages filled with empty promises. When you've been bought with the spotless blood of Jesus Christ, you are completely unaffordable for the devil.

God's Word should be the standard by which things in our lives are defined. We find beauty used in describing the Lord. He is beautiful. His presence is beautiful. Multitudes of people flocked and followed Jesus, the manifested God, wherever He went, in attempt to be in His presence. They just wanted to be close to Him. We don't know exactly what He looked like, but it really doesn't matter. Those who loved Him didn't care about the external. He was beautiful in their eyes because, beyond what any outward appearance could portray, they had seen the real genuineness and true nature of His deity. Even today, those who know Him in the power of His Spirit can say as the psalmist did:

One thing have I desired of the Lord, that will I seek after; that I may dwell in the house of the Lord all the days of my life, to behold the beauty of the Lord, and to enquire in his temple.
Psalm 27:4

Understanding the beauty of the Lord and all things connected to Him changes our perspective of real beauty. Beauty should be mirrored after Jesus. Anything against or contrary to Him should not be beautiful to us. It certainly is not beautiful to Him. If what we find beautiful is sexualized, artificial and contrary to godliness, then we fall short of pleasing God and even do ourselves a great disservice. If while striving to obtain beauty, we become self-absorbed and selfish, then we have wrongly misplaced our ambition and made cheap our own worth. If our quest becomes vicious and seductive, it is not real beauty to which we are headed. Beauty is the reflection of Jesus! Remember that laughable statement, "They have a great personality?" This is true. It's impossible to be more true. We all know someone of incredible character, meekness of spirit and fullness of joy who we undeniably see as beautiful and want to be around more.

Looks are not everything. They, of course, are important, but far from being supreme. Appearance tells the world who we belong to, who we love, and who we respect. As for me, I want the world to see that I belong to Jesus, that I love him. I love and respect my husband and others close to me, yet I respect myself. That is the highest honor. I believe, as Christians, we should take care of ourselves with respect and reverence for the beauty and likeness in which God made us in. Exercise and eat with self-control. It is just as much in Scripture as anything else:

> *What? know ye not that your body is the temple of the Holy Ghost which is in you, which ye have of God, and ye are not your own? For ye are bought with a price: therefore glorify God in your body, and in your spirit, which are God's.*
> *1 Corinthians 6:19-20*

I beseech you therefore, brethren, by the mercies of God, that ye present your bodies a living sacrifice, holy, acceptable unto God, which is your reasonable service.
Romans 12:1

It is not a ridiculous thing He has asked of us: it's reasonable. We are created for God, not to be objects for men or our bodies to be mere entertainment. How tragic for someone to be loved, in the very lowest possible sense of the word, for nothing more than their conjured up, outward appearance and not truly loved and admired for who their Creator created them to be. That is why we must "… come out from among them, and be ye separate, saith the Lord, and touch not the unclean thing; and I will receive you" (2 Corinthians 6:17). God desires for us to be separated from the world as witnesses; not justifying their sin with our own, but directing them toward Jesus with our lifestyle. They watch us; therefore, we need to look our best because we represent the best. We represent He Who is the answer to all of their problems. They may never look to the Bible for a description and definition of beauty, but daily they look to us.

THE UNDERSTANDING OF TRUE BEAUTY

The Hebrew word "glory" is synonymous with the word "beauty". Truly, the Glory of God and beauty are one and the same! When we say, "That is so beautiful," we are saying, "That is reflective of the glory of the Lord." As for me, that is the standard by which I deem something beautiful—does it reflect God's glory? What a convicting understanding. I pray we don't "oooh and ahh" over the beauty of sexual women or men. It grieves the heart of God when we have fallen into the trap that the beast of this world has laid for us. May we always see beauty the way God sees it.

It is funny how we can stare into the face of God's handiwork and admire the mountains of Colorado or stand speechless at the endless depths of the grand canyon and declare how beautiful they are, yet look into the mirror and say, "Eew, I am so ugly." Let us never forget that God makes all things beautiful, and we are His greatest creation.

> *So God created man in his own image, in the image of God created he him; male and female created he them.*
> *Genesis 1:27*

The fact that we are created in the image of God shows to us that we are beautiful as He is beautiful. Isaiah 33:17 says, "Thine eyes shall see the king in his beauty…"

Whatever the billboards and social media ads say, the King's way is beautiful. May the fear and lie of hell, that tells us God's standard of holiness in Scripture doesn't equate beauty, be defeated. Holiness and godliness are the purest forms of beauty. They are the essence of His identity and the thing in which He specializes: beauty. His beauty goes into the core of who we are as well. His beauty lasts forever and naturally draws people, along with their respect, to us in a way that mere empty, outward attraction could not. We are most beautiful when we are like Jesus, conformed to His image.

THE NATURE OF THE BEAST

What is the nature of the beast? The more you feed him, the

bigger he will grow. How true that is for the unattainable world of beauty and fashion. A new product, a new outfit, new make up, a little more edgy than last time is the progression that is taken. Every dollar spent feeds the beast, making him harder to control. Eventually, you are unable to stop the unrelenting lies and selfishness of obsession.

The goal of the fashion world is to rewire our God given ideal of beauty, by their imagery and carefully crafted marketing; redefining it for their agenda. The nature of the beast, Satan, is to be a false light and create false reality, twisting the very core of glory and what should be beautiful in our eyes. He tells us to be beautiful is to be sexy, ungodly, immodest, uncovered, stripped of submission to God, rebellious, self-centered, cheap and seductive. Satan says that as long as you do it all with glamor, you can get away with it and beauty shall be yours. The only problem is that it does not satisfy, which is always left out of the selling points. His bid sounds good but, at best, doesn't pay. He uses you for destruction until you have nothing left to destruct. The one who promised you love but only delivered lustful manipulation leaves you broken as he sets out to prey on his next victim. The one who peer-pressured you with that faithful line, "One drink won't hurt," is never there when alcohol singlehandedly destroys every one of your relationships. Misery loves company and hates self-control. There are no boundaries when one steps away from God's Word, making the pain and heartbreak boundless as well. Eventually, you are swallowed up by the ever-growing beast that you've faithfully fed for so long.

The world's beauty is self-centered, as is the beast. Beasts are always self-centered. You and I were created to be selfless, yet when we take on the nature of the beast we cannot truly feel satisfied or at peace with ourselves. We only find fulfillment, and the deepest sense of worth and beauty, when we conquer the beast and allow the manifested glory of God to radiate through our lives.

THE DESIRE FOR BEAUTY

The desire for beauty is not a bad thing. It is built into us by God to lead us to love. Theologian Augustine of Hippo said, "It is not possible to love what is not beautiful." Simply put, we do not love ugly things. It must be beautiful for us to love it. They say beauty is in the eye of the beholder, but what beauty is the beholder beholding? It's not the ugly; it's always the outer attractive shine and glimmer. Here's the catch: It is totally possible to possess what appears to be outward beauty, yet the inward parts of our heart be far from measuring up to outward false pretense that we portray.

In Matthew 23:27, Jesus speaks of the scribes and pharisees as having outward beauty yet inwardly ugly. Therefore, it matters not how beautiful one looks outwardly if they are ugly on the inside, with a nasty spirit and ugly attitude. True beauty is both within and without. Outward beauty, alone, is selfish. True beauty is not confined to a certain place, it permeates every area of who you are: inward and outward. Our motto and mission in striving to be like the Lord should be this: No ugly, just beauty.

FINDING BEAUTY

When you are beautiful, that beauty which glorifies God radiates and calls for respect without ever saying a word. It is the most accurate representation of Jesus and portrays through holy demonstration the beauty of God. In return, our lives are filled with unspeakable peace and contentment because our identity isn't in worldly affirmation but in the affirming power of God's Spirit.

Only godly beauty can satisfy. It does not expect or demand perfection, or any of the unattainable pressures that the fashion and cosmetic worlds call us to keep up with. When will we realize that we cannot keep up? They know that perfection is unattainable; therefore, satisfaction also has become an unreachable goal. How advantageous for them to always have a newer style, a better product or more trendy way to portray beauty. Give it time and, if you're honest with yourself, you will feel like a failure. That's the game. We chase the beast of beauty while, all along, the God who created us is waiting on our longing to align with His purpose and intentions for us. Does He not know us? Did He not give us His Word to lead and guide us? He gave us instruction, relationship and a plan for our salvation to be beautifully met. He gave us His presence where we see, through Him, ourselves as truly beautiful. He gave us the ability and responsibility to glorify Him. That's totally reasonable!

Thomas Aquinas, the Greek philosopher, defined three qualities that are found in everything beautiful: integrity, proportion, and clarity.

Integrity is in reference to wholeness. When women are portrayed as objects, their depth, value and nuance is lost. Partial things are not as pleasing to the human eye.

Proportion and symmetry were obsessions of ancient Greek sculptors. To master proportion is to master the quality of being made up of exactly similar parts facing each other or around an axis. Proper proportion is extremely attractive and pleasing to the eye. Babies spend more time staring at symmetrical pictures; men constantly rank women as most beautiful when symmetrical to the eye. Beyond that, disproportions are evident in the actions and character of our lives! Generous one day and cowardly the next, good one day and evil the next, that kind of disproportion isn't beauty at all.

Clarity is defined as a kind of radiance or splendor; the essence or core of someone or something, no pretenses, no make up, edits, falsities; just their essence. To be beautiful one must be whole in God, consistent daily in good character and radiant in the essence of who you are. All with which are virtually impossible to accomplish without Jesus.

Without His glory and time spent reflecting on Him, His Word and His character, we cannot be beautiful. We become who we spend time with, so I choose to spend time with Jesus. With distractions gone and our focus fixed on Jesus, we then understand true beauty. It is what is connected to Him, and nothing contrary to Him!

Jesus becomes our security, peace, joy, fulfillment, love, and confidence. He is our life more abundantly here and life eternal up there. In relationship with Him we come to know and experience true love, which sets the standard by which we live our lives. First knowing He who created us, we can then know ourselves. I know it goes against culture, but self-respect and self-love is totally attainable without make up, a new wardrobe and the magazine covers flawless figure. Don't misunderstand me. We must look nice and take care of ourselves. We are daughters of the King and should always look our best but not by covering ourselves up or making ourselves look cheap and buyable. In His presence, only, do we understand and see ourselves beautiful as He sees us. Through His eyes, you, my dear, are beautiful! You please Him most when you are like Him. That is true beauty.

God is within her, she will not fall; God will help her at break of day...
Psalm 46:5 (NIV)

She is clothed with strength and dignity; she can laugh at the days to come.
Proverbs 31:25 (NIV)

I will praise thee; for I am fearfully and wonderfully made: marvellous are thy works; and that my soul knoweth right well.
Psalm 139:14

To have a godly man look at you, as you uphold holiness and godliness, and tell you he sees you as beautiful is one of the greatest feelings a woman could feel; to be admired and complimented for the natural beauty of who she is and not what she is made up to be. I remember the moment Jeremy told me, for the first time, that I was beautiful. His eyes were misty as he took my hand, for what was also the first time. He had just asked me to be his girlfriend the night before and, moments later, would leave for a month. As I sat there amid the most romantic goodbye of my life, I heard him say "you look absolutely gorgeous." I was speechless. I am not normally at a loss for words, but it took me a few seconds to pick my jaw up from my lap and croak out the words "thank you." I had never felt more beautiful, confident or secure than I did in that moment. Since that day, that I hold so dear in my memory, I continue to feel that same sense of happiness and worth. It's as if that moment, which began it all, still lingers. I'll continue to do my best to look beautiful for my husband but, most of all, I pray that I am a true reflection of Jesus Christ and the beauty of His holiness.

the glory is always worth it

Because that, when they knew God, they glorified him not as God, neither were thankful; but became vain in their imaginations, and their foolish heart was darkened.
Romans 1:21

And changed the glory of the uncorruptible God into an image made like to corruptible man, and to birds, and fourfooted beasts, and creeping things.
Romans 1:23

We live in a world that is saturated in self-glory. The more beautiful, talented and accomplished one is, the more glory they are worthy of. The more sexualized you are, the more empowered you are. At least, that is what Hollywood says. I have observed this: it is only edited beauty that makes a Vogue cover. A voluptuous movie star is who makes the two page feature article in the magazine. The impressionable eyes, before which these mediums are placed, become obsessed with the name of one who is marketed as flawless. They are praised and glorified for their talent, looks and features; however, there is always more to their lives that what the photos show. If you dig enough you'll find those same idolized stars admitting to sleepless nights, every night, because of the demonic voices and tormenting lies that speak to them in the dark, midnight hours. In many cases, drugs become their escape and salvation, which leads to overdose and, in some situations, suicide.

These very people we place on pedestals will never prop up or promote awareness of the dangers and deadly issues that lie behind the cover story; dissatisfaction, loneliness, survival, hatred, depression and finding a drug to numb the pain of their own reality. The price they pay is a high cost for self-glory. We may have experienced a taste of these emotions as Christians, but we have a hope. We have a God who is our deliverer. Their god is themselves, and their only hope is a high of temporary escape.

> *Nevertheless among the chief rulers also many believed on him; but because of the Pharisees they did not confess him, lest they should be put out of the synagogue: For they loved the praise of men more than the praise of God.*
> *John 12:42-43*

That verse shakes me. To know there is more, yet refuse to confess Jesus because of a selfish love for the applause, approval and praise of men is frightening. When God enters into any equation, He in himself is the totality of all worth and value. For this reason, so many people emphatically reject God in their life so that all praise and glory can be centered around themselves. But, we were created to worship God; to live a life of selfless praise to Him and Him alone. The praise of men can make you feel good, but only until the lights go out and you are left with questions about your purpose and worth. Humanity was created for a purpose that is only found through selflessness.

Manufactured glory is a make-shift god, giving people a temporary satisfaction with deep rooted discontentment and misery. God aims to give us a lasting satisfaction and deep contentment, when we project the glory upwards. God specializes in knowing how to make our hearts happy, after all, he is the one who created us. It is so easy to look at a cover girl and think she has arrived and undoubtedly lives a fulfilled life. Oh, how often that is just not so. Who they really are and who we are is not told by what is on the outside, but inward: our character, integrity and heart.

I am somewhat intrigued by the stories and articles which expose the truth of how intensely miserable life beyond the limelight is for the music and movie stars of today. We often are enraptured with the beauty of a photoshopped woman or make-up covered model and fail to remember that there is a very real, stark, reality behind all the glamour and perfection you see. Once the blinders are taken off of our eyes and we be no longer deceived, we see how infallible the Word of God is pertaining to these things. Indeed, any pleasure offered of sin is only for a season.

Think about it, the viewers and readers may be deceived but the model is never duped. She is very familiar with the reality of who she is. How destructive it must be for her to constantly be confronted with the fact that, although she has been chosen for her beauty, so much editing and cover-up is necessary to meet the criteria of beauty's agenda. Their bodies are manipulated and reconstructed to scream at us, "This is the norm and this is how you should look." Some of the youngest Disney stars have admitted to experiencing intense anxiety and depression from the stress and pressure placed on them behind the scenes, yet they push themselves into more darkness than success because they don't want to let their audience down. Who would guess the pain they feel, when funny lines and laughable dialogue are recited for our entertainment? Humor is blinding and strategic. If we can laugh at something, we look past the fact that it was hurtful, inappropriate and even ungodly. It entertained us and put a smile on our face so what could be wrong with that? Honestly, there's plenty wrong with that. Our emotions should not be so easily submitted to things of an ungodly nature, funny or not. The Holy Ghost in us should detect, discern and then defeat the spirit and agenda of the world when it tries to seduce our hearts and minds. I pray that I am always conscious of what I am enjoying and what entertains me. Let only the things that please Jesus please me also.

The first chapter of Romans clearly addresses what we are facing right now. Our society has become just as was described by Paul, "... vain in their imaginations, and their foolish heart was darkened" (Romans 1:21).

Being filled with all unrighteousness, fornication, wickedness, covetousness, maliciousness; full of envy, murder, debate, deceit, malignity; whisperers, Back-biters, haters of God, despiteful, proud, boasters, inventors of evil things, disobedient to parents. Without understanding, covenant breakers, without natural affection, implacable, unmerciful:
Romans 1:29-31

We look at those things and think, "Wow, what a horrible person!" In fact, we would self-righteously proclaim of ourselves, "Thank God I'm not any of those things." However, though we be thankful for who we are not, there may be a little of all of us in those verses. The last verse brings it a little closer to home.

Who knowing the judgment of God, that they which commit such things are worthy of death, not only do the same, but have pleasure in them that do them.
Romans 1:32

In other words, those who approve and applaud those who practice these evil deeds are, in all reality, just at guilty of that same sin. You, yourself, may not personify what Paul described but what about the movies, shows and media you watch? I pray that we are convicted and not desensitized to how real this is. I want to be holy in all things. We cannot afford, as a soul winner and as a child of God bound for heaven, to be separated in our appearance yet watch and participate in evil behind closed doors. We cannot be hard on the world, yet watch the very things we condemn.

I am categorized as the "entertainer" in every personalty test I have taken. Stages, performances and acting are all things I love; however I have learned that using my talents for anything other than glorifying God will never bring true happiness or fulfillment. I have been drawn in by a performance and then later realized the ungodliness that it promoted. I had to discipline myself to take a step back and research what a song is actually saying. We fool ourselves into thinking there are not spirits attached. What a deceitful lie that is. I tell you this to show you that everyone is tempted and that we must draw the line of separation. The Apostles well understood the powers and principalities that fight against us, which caused Peter to write:

As he which hath called you is holy, so be ye holy in all manner of conversation. (1 Peter 1:15)

91

The Glory Is Always Worth it

I remember my mom telling me, "If Jesus walked into the room and saw what you were reading, looking at or watching, would He feel comfortable to take a seat and join you?" I have always remembered those words. We know Jesus is always with us, but it's seems to be forgotten and blocked out of our minds when participating in something contrary to His Word. We want Him on Sunday but not on Saturday? We want Him when we're tried but not when we're entertained? Is that how it is supposed to work? Not at all. There should be an all consuming passion for Him to be glorified at all times, in all we do. May the desire of God ever be to fellowship and commune with me, where He knows He'll always be reverenced and exalted. Nothing is worth Him walking out of my room.

Satan uses the element of attraction as a distraction: Attraction is distracting. Eve fell partly because of how attractive the fruit looked to her eyes. As the serpent (the devil) spoke, he used the tactic of distraction to disguise the evil that lay beneath the bite of that fruit. Oh, how we can be so easily fooled by the disguise of evil without ever considering the consequences which lay beneath what is being marketed for our consumption. I'm afraid sometimes we don't want to know the truth about these things. Is it because the truth might call us to change our ways? Truth might stir up conviction? There will be songs to skip over, books to throw out, shows to never be seen again. Attractive they may be, but they are just not worth the distraction. I pray for understanding and wisdom every day, along with reading God's word. Write down your thoughts and study the Scriptures out for yourself, and you will find His Word to be what attracts you most. Truly, it is the most beautiful thing we have. And you know what? The devil knows it! He knows what is beautiful and pure. He knows what is eternal and true. He knows that he cannot compare to the Word of God and the life it gives to us. So, with outward attraction, he masks death as life, pain as happiness and self-gain as glory.

If it is contrary to God's Word, it is not worth it. No show, no song, no humor is worth the distraction. God, convict us! May we never desire to waste our God-given gifts on this world or to glorify ourselves for a moment in the spotlight. The Bible pours truth onto this topic:

> *As they were increased, so they sinned against me: therefore will I change their glory into shame.*
> *Hosea 4:7*

> *For all flesh is as grass, and all the glory of man as the flower of grass. The grass withereth, and the flower thereof falleth away: But the word of the Lord endureth for ever. And this is the word which by the gospel is preached unto you.*
> *1 Peter 1:24-25*

SEEKING GOD'S GLORY

We must ask ourselves this question, "Am I seeking the glory of man or the glory of God?" It all comes down to your response to that self-evaluating question. As has already been mentioned, the Bible says "... that no flesh should glory in his presence" (1 Corinthians 1:29). God is a jealous God and will also not share His glory with another; therefore, when self is exalted above Him, He will simply remove His presence from our lives. That scares me! The thought of God's protective power and peaceful presence being absent from my life, my home, my church, my conversation and my career is a terrifying fear. I am my own protector when God leaves, and I am not strong enough to fight off the evil forces that daily bombard our hearts and minds. Therefore, I daily desire and welcome His presence to dwell with me and in me. In no way do I want to shut God out of my life. In fact, very few people actually outright tell God to leave. Most just simply crowd Him out and invite other spirits whom God will not strive or compete with. But as for me, I want the glory of His presence. Above all else and before anything else, I choose Him and Him alone.

What beautiful words did the Apostle Paul write, which sum it all up:

If I must needs glory, I will glory of the things which concern mine infirmities.
2 Corinthians 11:30

If I glory in anything at all, it will be my weakness, because when I am weak, He is strong. When I have nothing, He truly is my everything! Therefore, it really is all about Jesus. In His presence you want for nothing of yourself, only more of Him.

THE DEFINITION

To see God's Glory is to see the fullness of God, or all of Him. I can't help but think of Moses when, in God's presence, He begged these words: "I beseech thee, shew me thy glory" (Exodus 33:18).

He was already in conversation with God, already in His presence, and with all of that goodness surrounding him, Moses wanted more. Thankful, but yet he was still unsatisfied until all of God was revealed unto Him. I am intrigued by the response of our Lord unto Moses.

> *I will make all my goodness pass before thee, and I will proclaim the name of the LORD before thee; and will be gracious to whom I will be gracious, and will shew mercy on whom I will shew mercy.*
> *Exodus 33:19*

To see all of God in His fullness is to see His goodness, His mercy, His grace and the power of His Name. That is the very essence of Who our God is.

The enemy of our soul understands the power of a life lived under submission to God. That life is met with the favor of God and His manifold blessings. It is a selfless and holy life. The opposite is also true; when we glory only in ourselves, our works and our accomplishments, life is then met by an enemy who seeks to devour. Therefore, it can be said that your relationship with God, or the lack thereof, determines whether God is glorified by your life or if all the glory is directed toward you.

Fascinating is the dialogue between Jesus and the rich young ruler who wanted to be saved. Jesus told him the first six commandments, which pertained to human relationships. He didn't struggle with those! However, when Jesus got to the other four, which required a submitted walk with God, he realized that he couldn't handle those. Unwilling to align himself with God's commandments, this young man walked away having made a tragic choice. He had all potential of living a life full of God's glory, yet chose to remain ruler of His own kingdom and glory in his own self. Accepting a partial portion of God is unacceptable. We must choose all of Him or nothing at all. When we choose all of Him, we undoubtedly will see His glory revealed in us.

GLORY IN THE CHURCH

The dwelling or settling place of God was referred to in Hebrew as the Shekinah glory. The holy place of the Old Testament tabernacle was dedicated to the sole purpose of the Shekinah glory coming down. There was, and even still is, absolutely nothing like the glory of God settling down into a place made holy by prayer, praise and sacrifice. When Jesus makes His presence known, it's undeniable.

At seventeen years of age, I saw the Shekinah glory of God. Perhaps that sounds unbelievable to you, but it was beyond believable to me as I visibly beheld it with my own eyes. It was a supernatural experience to say the least. Months earlier, my prayer had been to see something supernatural of God. I was hungry for it. An evangelist had come to our church for a weekend revival, and I remember one particular service being exceptionally powerful. God was moving so strongly that the service agenda was swept away by the glory of God that filled the sanctuary. We didn't need another song, we only needed to hear what the Spirit was saying to the church.

A friend from my high school was at the altar weeping in the over-whelming presence of God. A broken family was also in the altar praying together, arms lovingly around each other as God restored every hurtful word and bitter scene from their home. No other words better describe it than to say, this is the power of God. The pain and resentment toward their alcoholic father was obliterated there in the presence of God.

I was standing in the back of the sanctuary. The back right corner was where I always prayed during pre-service prayer. More than just a routine, it was special to me. There I stood in awe of how real the presence of God was, and I had one prayer: "Lord, show me something deep in the Spirit realm. Give me just a glimpse so I can feel that much closer to you." You must understand that my request wasn't made out of doubt. It was completely out of faith! He had healed me many times, and I had seen undeniable miracles. I already felt so close to Him, but I just wanted more. Raw hunger and childlike faith brought me to the point of asking that same question of Moses: "God, show me your glory."

Therefore I say unto you, What things soever ye desire, when ye pray, believe that ye receive them, and ye shall have them.
Mark 11:24

Interestingly enough, some of the most spiritually powerful and epoch moments in my life were when evangelists came to our church. Now, as the evangelist's wife I always wanted to be, I walk into churches where sometimes hundreds and sometimes only a handful gather to worship. When I see youth groups of one or two young people, I know exactly how they feel. Although to them I am a guest, I often feel right at home because I've been where they are. Sure, it's a different city, state and church name, but loneliness is loneliness wherever you are. And so, to those who I see my teenage self in, I want to encourage. I feel as if God has called me, in part, to pour into them and be "that evangelist's wife" in their lives who took time to care about them. Undoubtedly, many of them also have prayed the same prayers as I: "God, I just want to see your glory."

It was just a few weeks into my junior year at Moose Lake High School, my first year attending public school. I remember going to school on Monday morning, following that weekend revival, expecting to visibly see an angel with me. I was sure that would be the glimpse God would give me. In fact, I was so sure that I confidently wrote in my journal the night before that I would see an angel with me at school. Would you believe, nothing happened? October passed. November. December. Still nothing. Week after week, I would drive to our church straight from school and, while kneeling at the altar, pray this prayer again and again: "God, show me something supernatural." It was important to me, so important that I wouldn't let it go, yet still I saw nothing.

Time passed and somewhere in the midst of the compiled months, I eventually forgot my heartfelt prayer. Suddenly the school year had come to a close, and the freedom of summer days and camp season was at hand. It was somewhat of a lonely time in my life, away from the busyness of the school year. I attended Thursday night of Minnesota family camp, where I had the privilege of sharing my testimony and singing the song I wrote about God's healing. Following my song, I sat down in the audience and the camp evangelist stepped to the pulpit to preach. I didn't catch every word he said, because something else had caught my eye. I saw what looked like a blue haze. I saw it only for a second, but I knew in my heart that it was holy. I prayed "Lord, if that is you showing me something, show me again." Again, just for a second, I saw it. I prayed the same prayer again and a third time I saw it: now closer this time than before. Immediately I knew what it was. My mind recalled a story that my mom had told me about my Grandma Apker seeing the Shekinah glory of God at a camp meeting years ago in Wisconsin. She described it as a blue mist. Could it be? Oh yes, it could. I felt the Holy Ghost was so strong that, right there in the middle of everything, I bowed my head and began weeping. As if this moment wasn't already impacting enough, I then heard the voice of God say, "The reason you did not see this in your school is because my glory is not in your school, it is in the church."

It was so clear and real that I wept in awe of God's timing and power. Eight months had passed and I was sure that God had forgotten my prayer. I had forgotten my prayer! Yet, I was reminded again that God never forgets our prayers and although He doesn't always answer as quickly as we'd like, He does answer in His perfect timing. God knew I needed the answer more then than ever.

God's glory is in the church. It isn't in the sin infested hallways of a high school, it's in the church. I knew that His presence goes with us when we live pure and holy lives, but I needed to hear those confirming words of where God shows forth the fullness of Himself.

Why do people, living a life of sin, stay so far from the church? Why do they avoid the temple of God? It's not the building, the pastor or the people that they ultimately avoid. It's the glory of God that they steer away from. As did Adam and Eve in the garden of

Eden, so do they hide from Him in shame. They know that inside the four walls of a sanctuary they will feel Him and be convicted and changed. If you stop and think about it, it's a beautiful thought for the heart that follows after God. Toward His glory we run! Yet, for the rebellious sinner who willfully flees His presence, it is tragically terrifying.

> *Unto him be the glory in the church... throughout all ages, world without end.*
> *Ephesians 3:21*

Clovis Chappell wrote in his book, *Feminine Faces*:

"The scene is the temple of Jerusalem. Jesus has gone to church. That was his constant custom. The church of that day was at a low ebb spiritually. Many of it's members were leading mean and unworthy lives. Its services were doubtless often quite cold and barren and dead. But Jesus never took the position that He could worship just as well outside the church. He believed that he could meet God in the church in spite of the failures of his fellows. He also believed that he could give something to the church in its hour of need. It never occurred to him to try to improve the spiritually impoverished church of his day by merely letting it alone. He made a business of attending church."

Jesus is in the church! Even while some numbered among the church crowd be hypocritical and ungodly, that didn't keep Jesus away. That is not at all an approval of hypocrisy or ungodliness.

We all should strive to be like Jesus and lessen our likeness of this world; however, we also can't expect the people who gather inside the walls of our churches to all be perfect. How foolish it is to say, "A lot of people in the church are hypocrites, so I'm not going to church." How foolish to use the faults of others as a means of justifying your own. Clearly, it isn't Christ-like at all. People or problems never kept Jesus from going to the temple! Jesus said, "... where two or three are gathered together in my name, there am I in the midst of them" (Matthew 18:20). It doesn't matter who is there and what their life looks like, I just want to gather in His name knowing that He will show up.

In the Old Testament, the Lord commanded that their tents face the tabernacle, the church, for that was where the glory of the Lord dwelt. Oh, how beautiful is the thought that they would wake up and throw back the tent flap and look toward the glory of God. The Tabernacle was the portable dwelling place of Yahweh (God) for the children of Israel, and their lives were centered around this sacred place. With our lives being no different, we should wake up every morning, in our own dwelling places, having Jesus at the center of our existence. How can I possibly use passing words to expound upon the eternal truth of just how important it is to put God first and foremost in our lives? It is a taste-and-see experience. Until you've dwelt in the shadow of the almighty, you may not understand. For me, the beauty of our home is not the fact that it is an RV, nor is it the revolving view out our window from week to week as we move from campgrounds to church parking lots. The real beauty of our home is that we have placed Christ at the center. I see that reflected when I look at my husband and see Him searching through Scripture, praying for God's perfect will and constantly endeavoring to further himself in knowledge of the Word. Even when the motorhome is long gone, that longing in our hearts to pursue God and put Him first will remain. May His Glory be evident in our home and wherever we go. Even, when we visit a hotel, resort or an Airbnb, it is no different. Wherever our dwelling place may be, we daily awake and look toward Him to see His glory.

God has always made a way to meet with His people. From the wilderness tabernacle to the carefully constructed temples in Scripture, and now the New Testament church that was born on the day of Pentecost, God always made sure that we could get to Him and He to us. Church is important to God, and it must be important to us. To truly seek after the glory in our lives, means we must have a church in our lives. A place where we are submitted to the man of God, a place where our praises go up and glory comes down, a place where we are ministered to by the Word and presence of God, a place where we pray fervently, a place where we come together as the body of Christ.

Think of this, as incredible as feeling His presence is on any given Sunday at your church or even in your home daily, it is only a small foretaste of glory divine. It's wonderful, no doubt, but compared to heaven, where we will bask in the pure uninterrupted presence of God for ever, Sunday morning service is just a little sample. To feel his glorious presence eternally is something our minds cannot fully comprehend, until our incorruptible bodies bow before His throne in the new Jerusalem. That is the real grandeur of His presence: heaven. The streets of gold like unto pure glass will be quite the sight, but nothing will measure up to the unexplainable feeling of peace, joy and wonder when we shall behold Him just as He is.

In Revelation 21:22, John was on the island of Patmos when he beheld a vision of heaven. While trying to put into words what awaits us, he writes, "And I saw no temple therein: for the Lord God Almighty and the Lamb are the temple of it." There we will not need to gather in a certain building with a steeple and sign out front. He is the temple! While earthly dwelling places serve us well down here, His eternal dwelling place we will have reached. Oh, what a day that will be! It will be worth every earthly struggle when we finally see Jesus.

THE EFFECTS OF HIS GLORY

Deep in the presence of the Lord, you see the ugliness of sin and the beauty of godliness. When the contrast is made clear between the two, one cannot help but long to attain holiness and righteousness, like unto our Holy God. You want to be filled with Him. You want to be like Him. After Isaiah saw the throne room of heaven, where one sat on the throne, and heard the inquiring voice of God ask for whom He may send, Isaiah said "here I am Lord, send me." He had seen God's glory, which brought forth a hunger and willingness to be used by God. If our lives really do glorify God, we will be known by this one thing: Our lives will reveal His glory to the world. Everyone will see Jesus in us.

Three months after Jeremy and I were married, my back became the source of the worst pain I have ever experienced. I visited a new chiropractor who, unfortunately, re-injured an old previous injury, making the pain almost unbearable. Two days later, in a service at a minister's conference in Oklahoma, God separately spoke to me and my husband and told us that he was taking us through this for us to get closer to Him and to be used by Him in a greater way. I realized on the way home from that service that Jesus suffered pain for glory. If He did, why wouldn't I? In pain, we must not get bitter or angry and despise the day of trouble. We must praise Him every step of the way. Through our suffering, God is faithful and will sustain us. Others will see, through out trouble, just how mighty God is. Paul said in Romans 8:18, "For I reckon that the sufferings of this present time are not worthy to be compared with the glory which shall be revealed in us."

So, if you want to see the Glory of the Lord, then the question must be asked: where are you looking? It won't be seen in this world; therefore, we must know where to look for it.

But he, being full of the Holy Ghost, looked up stedfastly into heaven, and saw the glory of God.
Acts 7:55

We must look up! Turn your attention away from this world's fads and fashionable trends. Look skyward and allow heaven to come down to you. Trust me, the glory of God is always worth it.

CHAPTER SEVEN

a changing time

The excitement of freshman year at one's dream college is a monumental moment in anyone's life. Personally, I loved that jittery feeling of meeting hundreds of new peers. Trying to make your dorm room as home-like as possible when home is so far away. The classes seem exciting until you experience the dread of assignment deadlines and mounting homework that, in retrospect, you're not sure how you completed. On the other hand, how exciting it is to adventure through a new big city and discover coffee shops and cupcake bakeries with new friends. It was nothing short of joyous for me. I thrived in the excitement of a new environment. Not only were the setting and circumstances around me new, but it was as if the future before me had been seen in a new light. I was on my way to becoming something for the Lord.

I had worn out every CD of them that I owned. I am responsible for many of their high number of views on YouTube. I attended a live recording while still in high school and dreamingly looked the platform over, searching for a place where I, myself, hoped and dreamed to fit in just a few long years later. They slowly passed and following high school graduation, I packed my Impala and chased down the reality of my long-awaited ambition.

A Changing Time

Finally, I was a student at the illustrious Indiana Bible College.

I took in every moment: the vocal tryouts, the classes, chapel services, student body prayer. Oh, student body prayer. Things change when you get a group of Holy Ghost filled young adults together, everything else set aside, calling on the name of the Lord.

The first Tuesday night student body prayer of the year would prove to be a night that would change my life. I tucked myself away in a corner with the Lord and remember specifically telling God how happy I was to be there. I also asked God not to let anything happen to my family while I was away. It was a fear that I just could not bear. I had heard so many stories of young people who followed the will of God for their lives, deciding to give up other plans and dreams to follow His call, and the enemy tried his antics to stop them from turning their world upside down for Jesus Christ with apostolic anointing and truth. My family was everything and I feared what my horror story might be, yet God gave me peace. After that night, I almost forgot about my prayer and even my fear.

MY PROMISE TO GOD

My first IBC live recording, as a student, surpassed all expectations. I had never experienced anything like standing amid hundreds of like-minded peers, exalting the one true God and feeling His glorious presence settle down into that sanctuary. It was truly what I had dreamed of and, making it all the more special, my family had driven down from Minnesota to be there. My sister Aimee and I have always been extremely close, even though she's almost five years younger than me. We were playmates most of the time but best friends always. She is intellectual when I am clueless. She is sarcastic when I am sincere. She is a straight thinker when I'm an emotional feeler. She is her own person, and I admire her.

We had not seen each other in months, so there was much excitement the day following the live recording when we sat down together for a wonderful meal at my favorite restaurant. To our surprise, Aimee woke up very sick the next morning. We first assumed it was food poisoning, but we'd all eaten the same thing, and the rest of us were fine. She stayed at the hotel all weekend, too sick to go anywhere. It was a disappointment, but none of us were overly concerned. On Sunday afternoon my parents and sister departed Indianapolis and embarked upon the twelve hour road trip home, my sister being violently sick the whole way home. I panicked when I received that call that she'd blacked out in the bathroom of a roadside rest stop. When they arrived home, they took her to the doctor, and she was admitted to the hospital. Their claim was that she was very low on fluids and iron. Once hydrated, she was sent home, and we expected Aimee to immediately bounce back to her typical self.

Over the next few days, although she was home, she only grew worse. She couldn't eat or sleep. I remember being twelve hours away in my Indianapolis dorm room reading her texts. I could tell she was afraid, but I couldn't be there with her. After no improvements in her condition, my parents took her back to the emergency room, this time getting a CAT scan. While awaiting the results of the scan, my family was discharged but advised to stay near the hospital until they received a call concerning the test results. While sitting anxiously waiting for some answers and, of course praying, the doctor called. Her appendix had burst ten days prior and he

109

said, "We must do surgery immediately." My phone rang with the news. I was relieved that an answer had been found, but now all the more fearful for my little sister. My body was shaking. I was too scared to cry. This was family! Nothing was supposed to happen to my family! In that moment, none of us knew what the outcome would be.

Of all nights, it was a Tuesday night. At the exact time Aimee was being rolled into the operating room in that Moose Lake hospital, I was walking into our weekly student body prayer meeting. I found my way back to that same familiar corner where I had prayed on the very first Tuesday night of the semester. As I knelt down I hardly knew what to pray. "Oh, God you can't take her! She is the closest thing to me. I can't bear it." I pleaded with God over and over to keep angels around her. I pleaded and prayed that she'd be okay. I exercised every ounce of faith that I could find, even in my desperate and paralyzed state. I called on the name of Jesus and then, I made a promise. In His presence, curled up in the corner of that chapel, I prayed "God, please spare my sister, but no matter what happens, I will still serve you faithfully". It was a struggle to get out those words between heavy sobs, but I said it. and I meant it.

For the next 40 minutes of student body prayer, I didn't pray another word. All I could do was weep. There were two reasons for my tears: I realized how deep my love was for my sister but also how deep my love was for the God that I served. The same God I served was the same God Aimee served. He'd been faithful to me, and He would be faithful to her. I realized that night, and all the more since, that we must never allow the circumstances of life to alter our devotion to God. Every circumstance, good or bad, should make stronger that devotion.

When my sister came out of surgery, the surgeon told my dad "There were angels looking out for her." He went on to inform my parents that Aimee's intense sickness was caused by abscesses in her intestines that were filled with poison and infection, which He had removed in surgery. He was very honest, "Mr. and Mrs. Reece, your daughter should have been dead." It had been ten days since her appendix had unknowingly burst back in Indiana. God had kept her, and her life, more than ever before, is a miraculous testimony to the power of God.

Following surgery she faced two weeks in the hospital to insure that all of the infection drained out of her system. By the second day I couldn't handle the distance any longer and made a surprise trip to see her. I will never forget the sight of my loving mother combing out her hair in the hospital room when I walked in. Aimee, who looked so pale and fragile, was so touched that I had come. Tears, tears, tears. Happy tears. Everything was finally okay, and we were together. I wouldn't leave the hospital that night. I laid there with her in the hospital bed, and many of our relatives came to see her. Miraculously, it was just a few more days before the infection was gone, and she was able to go home.

I was in awe once again by God's miraculous hand and love for His children. He always protects those who serve Him and live according to His Word. How lovely and safe it is to be close to the all powerful God! He is walking faithfully with us, even when we do not see Him or His foot-prints. But sometimes, in hindsight, God does allow us to see the evidence of IIis faithful in our dark hours. One year later in a family camp service at Camp Galilee in Minne-

111

sota, God spoke separately to my parents and said, "The enemy tried to take her, but I wouldn't let him." Comparing notes later they realized that God had allowed them to glance back over that dark time and see His footprints. He was in the middle of it all; leading, guiding, protecting and keeping.

Oh, how the enemy tries to take out the child of God. Jesus called him a thief who "... cometh not, but for to steal, and to kill, and to destroy" (John 10:10). He comes in like a flood, but we know how to pray. We know who to turn to, we know whose Name holds all power. At the mention of the Name of Jesus, the efforts and force of the enemy is not only held back but defeated. Isaiah 59:19 says, "... the Spirit of the Lord shall lift up a standard against him." God is able to put to flight every enemy that comes against you! He is far greater than our adversary, and He holds all power in heaven and in earth. As for me, I will never be content anywhere but in the safety of being close to the one who is in control.

THE QUESTION FROM GOD

After Aimee's miracle story had unfolded, she bounced back to normal, and life moved on for all of us. Back at IBC there soon came MusicFest in April of that year. I was so excited, particularly to have been asked to be a background vocalist for an artist who was doing a live recording during one evening's concert. Opportunities and moments like these were what my dreams were filled with. On that night it was no longer a dream; it was actually happening! Yet, simultaneous with my excitement was also a strange sense of conflict within. Before walking onto the platform, I knew something was deeply troubling me, but I did not know how and couldn't put my finger on what. Nevertheless, it was time to walk onto the platform. The lights beamed down upon us, blinding us from seeing much of anything or anyone in the audience. With the microphone in my hand as I waited for the song to start, I suddenly heard the almost audible voice of God ask me a question: "If you were never on a platform again, would you still serve me?"

I was stunned. What a question! My first instinctive answer was to say "Yes, of course, God." The song started, and I had to focus on the song, singing as though everything was fine, but in my heart I could not wait to walk off that platform and talk with God. I can't tell you how long I stayed around the altar, but I can tell you that the altar changed my life that night. You see, from a young age I had been blessed to sing many places and on many platforms. It was, quite honestly, my comfort zone. It was exciting and fulfilling! I sung for Jesus, and His presence always came down, so my passion was to let others feel what I felt. Singing was my world, but that night God was doing something in my heart. God was desiring for me to be as passionate about Him as I was the gifts and talents He'd given me.

In brokenness and tears I told God that I would finish the few short weeks of that current semester, but sit myself down for the next six months. I would not be on one platform, no matter who asked me to sing. I committed to the Lord that I would still serve Him, even if there were no more platforms to stand on or microphones to hold. It wasn't some flippant prayer and meaningless commitment prayed in an emotional moment: I meant it. I wanted to show God, not just with words but with action, that I loved Him from the bottom of my heart. I could've answered His question with a simple "yes" and moved on, but my heart could not hurry away from His voice. Action was necessary on my part. As Abraham showed himself willing to offer the closest thing to Him—his son— as a sacrifice unto the Lord on Mount Moriah, I also felt compelled to scale the heights of a hard commitment and prove that I was willing to take the hard road of sacrifice in order to please the Lord. I had no idea what the next six months would bring or be like, but it didn't matter. I felt the affirming presence of God flood my soul in that altar. I was truly on holy ground. Sure, I knew there would be challenges, temptation and moments of frustration, but this would be the next season of my life. After all, if God was leading me into it then God would lead me through it. As extreme and, perhaps, naive as it might sound, I knew I could handle hardship and trial as long as I was in the Will of God. Unable to get up from underneath the weight of God's glory, I told the Lord "It is not about the spotlight; it is all about you, Jesus. I will serve you faithfully without a platform. I don't need to sing before a crowd, I don't need the limelight, I just need you!"

I told no one of this moment, outside of my parents who were my spiritual covering. It was so intimate and real that I couldn't share it with friends yet. They might not understand. They weren't there. They didn't have the experience I had in that altar. You should never be ashamed of moments on holy ground between you and the Lord. Don't ever think that your personal encounter with God must be validated by the opinions of others. Always have an open line of communication with your spiritual covering but have confidence in what the voice of the Lord has said and what you have felt in His presence.

Here is the reality. That divine, holy encounter happened within one evening, yet living out my commitment would take an entire six months. When you compare one evening to the span of six months, the contrast is stark. Could what happened in a few hours sustain me through a whole half year? The skeptic says no, but the one who is convinced of God's faithfulness says yes. I knew the months ahead would be trying and that on some days it would be easy to compromise the covenant I made. There were certainly times that I wondered where God went. His presence wasn't always as clearly evident as it had been that night in the altar, but I made sure my commitment was. I refused to blur the lines or make exceptions. If God confirms His Word and never compromises a promise made to us, then shouldn't I do the same with my words given to Him? As we take His Word seriously, He takes ours seriously also.

Nevertheless I will remember my covenant with thee in the days of thy youth, and I will establish unto thee an everlasting covenant.
Ezekiel 16:60

The moment of commitment held value, not only to me, but to God also. He took account of my words and, pending their fulfillment and my faithfulness to them, God formed my future and divinely orchestrated steps of favor and blessing that I will one day take. God always honors those who are faithful to honor Him and their commitments to Him.

Have you had a God moment? A moment where you know without any doubt that God has spoken to you? Have you heard that whispering voice ask the question that could change your life for the better, if you humbly respond? Perhaps you've heard that voice and felt His drawing on multiple occasions but you've been too caught up with your own spot-light that you have dismissed it. I challenge you to listen for His voice and obey. It can be scary and uncertain to step out of your comfort zone and commit yourself to God, but seeing the unfolding wonder of His will is worth it all.

The plan that God has for you is beautiful. I pray you answer His call and obey His voice. We are safe in Him, no matter what the circumstances look like, and we can trust Him.

CHAPTER EIGHT

no platforms. just altars

Because of finances and the promise I'd made to God of not being on a platform for six months, my parents and I decided it best to take a semester off from college. Let me be real, I am 100% extrovert. I need people. I need to talk! Being around people and conversing with them is what gives me energy and purpose. It gives me life!

After the close of that previous semester I came home and had so many questions about not only my future but my present. Where would I work since I would be home for more than just a short summer break? What would I do not leading worship or playing the piano at church? More importantly, what weighed most on me was the uncertainty of how lonely I was about to feel. I was so used to seeing friends, attending classes and bouncing from one social event to the next. Now, for at least the next 7 months, it was all gone.

Being a pastor's kid from a small church presented many opportunities for involvement, not only in Moose Lake but even in our district. I had led worship nearly every Sunday from the age of fourteen and been privileged to sing at youth events across Minnesota. My sister Adina and I got to sing at the Minnesota State Fair one year, as well as the county fair and other community events. Beyond Minnesota, I had been privileged to travel across several states with a small music group from IBC during my first year of college. Needless to say, music and ministry was a part of me. I thrived on learning new songs, practicing parts, being involved with a team of musicians and then ministering through those songs. Yet, here I was. For now, I could see all of that only in the rear view mirror.

Did I make a mistake? Did I miss the will of God? Was that commitment unnecessary? Did I only get caught up in the emotion of the moment and speak out of impulse? I could try to rationalize and reason away my commitment and seeking justification of a compromise, but would I be able to live with myself? Even in the drudge of daily routine, I'd rather live with the clear conscience that I was faithful to He who has been so faithful to me. God never goes back on His promises toward us, and I never want to go back on mine toward Him. Any time you are forced beyond your comfort zone you will be most uncomfortable. Uncomfortableness often leads people to extreme measures of coping; therefore, you must remain true to God and to yourself. In trying times, your true character will always be revealed. Not who you think you are, or who people think you are, but who you really are. It is your identity and self-disciplines that prepare you for the defining moments of life. So the question must be asked: are you prepared? Daily prayer, devotion and worship are those training grounds on which we make ourselves ready to fight the battles that come against us. Oh, what a battle I was about to fight.

They were new words in my vocabulary: anxiety and depression. When that first anxiety attack hit me like a ton of bricks, I quite literally had no idea what was happening. I was driving and remember not being able to catch my breath. My throat was closing up and my consciousness was trying to slip away from me behind the dark cloud of an unfathomable fear. Although I didn't understand the fullness of what was happening, I refused to let myself give in to this strange feeling. Shaking uncontrollably, I reached for my phone and called my mom. If I could just talk to her, I thought I would be okay. Her kindness is always so reassuring and comforting, which was exactly what I needed in that moment. Our conversation helped, and I was able to calm down, but the trauma of that experience had a residual effect that lingered all day.

No one can truly comprehend what this is like unless you've experienced it yourself. It is all consuming. Your one desire is that this dark presence would free your mind and emotions so you can enjoy life again. I never understood that before this day. In fact, I was always at a loss when someone spoke of anxiety or depression. To be perfectly honest, in my ignorance, I thought they just needed to pray. I thought, perhaps, they weren't close enough to God, but then, according to my own logic, my closeness to God was brought into question. What I thought I would never face, I now stood face to face with. Anxiety is no respecter of persons.

Very shortly, I interviewed for a position and was hired. The job required working in a nice home, interacting with disabled adults. I could thrive in this! A cozy home, human interaction and the reward of making a difference all gave me much excitement. I was encouraged and relieved to see everything falling into place.

My first day on the job was perfect until I had another one of those dreaded attacks. Trying to cover it up, I told my co-worker I needed to step outside to get some air. I stepped outside and began to pray. I felt a little peace but was still scared. I always knew I could handle anything with Jesus, but this was so different than anything I had faced before. For the next several days following, I felt extreme heaviness and loneliness.

Out of shear fear one day, I went to a walk-in medical clinic after work. When the doctor came in the room I explained what these attacks felt like. I just needed to know I was going to be okay! I needed to know I wasn't the only one who had struggled with this. Unfortunately, the doctor was not as empathetic as I'd hope she would be. She immediately offered to write me a prescription for anxiety medicine. She seemed so insensitive and ready to move on to her next patient. I wanted to be hurt by her carelessness, but yet before I knew it something had risen up within me. Yes, I was struggling and looking for answers, but I was not taking medicine for this. Some may, and I believe that it is sometimes necessary, but I felt like treating my anxiety with medication was to accept it as my own possession. For me, that wasn't an option. I would not claim this. Although I had to put up with it temporarily, I refused to possess it permanently. "I will be fine," I told the doctor and left the clinic. I am sure she was confused as to why I had come looking for help, yet was so quick to leave with her prescription unfilled. I didn't want medicine, I wanted someone to tell me I would be okay. I wanted someone to tell me I wasn't alone and that I could overcome this. My emotionally connected self needed to hear a happy story of someone who'd felt the very things I had felt and overcame them.

The days crept by slowly. When friends would visit our home, I found myself tucked in bed with no desire to get up and go visit. That was not characteristic of me at all. If you know me then you can understand the unusualness of such behavior. I loved when people came to our home! We always cooked food, baked cookies and between four-wheeling, snowmobiling, riding scooters or playing ping-ping, we would have plenty of fun. Yet, as unusual as it was, I just couldn't bring myself to be around people. My dad came up to check on me, inquiring as to why I hadn't come down. I stood in front of him, and all I could do was sob. I was not okay.

The next week my mom and sister attended a youth event and didn't return home until late into the night. I chose to stay home, which is so uncharacteristic to my personality. I love going and doing; however, on the occasions where I am home alone, I am the girl who bangs on the piano and sings at the top of her lungs, eats all the chocolate chips in the house because no one is there to judge and takes walks down our country road. That day was different. All I wanted to do was stay curled up in bed, unmoved from an all consuming fear and dreadful dullness. I couldn't sleep, but I couldn't get out of bed either. In my own home, the most peaceful place I knew, I felt afraid for no apparent reason. When my mom got home at two o'clock in the morning, I crawled in bed with her, sobbing—"I can not do this anymore, mom. This isn't me. This isn't living!"

My mom pulled out a piece of paper filled with Scriptures from underneath her pillow. Yes, that is how amazing she is. I am so thankful for a godly mother. "Jamin," she said, "all these Scriptures are about fear. God is not the author of fear, so we are going to pray His Word out loud."

There we laid in her bedroom reading and praying the Scriptures out loud repeatedly with authority. We prayed with desperation and fervency until something broke. God's presence flooded that bedroom, and my mom and I began speaking in tongues. I had been filled with the Holy Ghost for the first time at the age of seven and had been refilled count-less times since then, but how refreshing it was in that very moment for the river of living water to well up inside me once again. I am so thankful for the gift of the Holy Ghost; it is just that, a precious heavenly gift. James 1:17 says, "Every good gift and every perfect gift is from above."

> *But ye shall receive power, after that the Holy Ghost is come upon*
> *you....*
> *Acts 1:8*

I will never take for granted the opportunity of knowing this powerful truth and having the precious experience of being with His Spirit. It gives us great power against the adversary of our soul and his attacks. As the power of the Holy Ghost was activated by faith mixed with the Word of God, we truly felt angels come into that bedroom. Since that moment, which made such an impact on my faith, anxiety and depression have never controlled my life for even a moment. I learned that day how to use the power of God's Word and Spirit to combat the enemy.

I understand timing is different for everyone who struggles with it, but one thing is the same: do not give up. Do not quit fighting! You will feel like yourself again, and you will be okay. Please do not condemn yourself, your faith or your relationship with God. Do not be afraid to reach out to someone for help and admit you are not okay. That completely goes against what a person feels like doing when dealing with anxiety, fear and depression, but forcing yourself to open up to someone who can pray with you and build up your faith is what will bring about your deliverance. If you pray for deliverance without seeing your prayer answered and need medicine, then get medicine. It is okay to get help! People and prescriptions can never replace God, but they can be used by Him to help you. Most importantly, don't ever stop praying! You will find prayer to be your strength and greatest weapon. Prayer will combat the odds that stack against you and call into fulfillment the purpose and plans that God has for you. It is never His will for you to give up!

Life has no meaning when you feel as though you are not living. Though you may breathe air in and out, if there is an absence of joy, purpose and passion, then life can hardly seem worth living. We can be comforted by the fact that God understands. He always understands and has given His Word to sustain us. As if to throw a line of rescue in our direction that we might grasp hold of and cling to, Jesus said in John 10:10, "The thief cometh not, but for to steal, and to kill, and to destroy: I am come that they might have life, and that they might have it more abundantly." It is one of my favorite Scriptures. I love being full of life! In fact, due to my personality type, I am often one of those referred to as "the life of the party." Joy, happiness and enthusiasm is what I thrive on and, although personality types are real, I understand that there is more to my joy than just a personality type. He is my joy! He is the source of the over-flowing life inside of me. The joy that I express is nothing more than the overflow of what God has given unto me within. Although it seems less than profound, I am convinced of the truth that you cannot give what you do not have. The same is for our God: He is joy, in its very essence, which is why He can give it in such abundance! What contrast is given to our mind's eye through those words of Jesus. His description of the thief's mission calls to our mind a lost world who daily cope their way through life, living for their next high and looking for their next temporary thrill. They live lives without purpose or promise, yet Jesus then offers great hope to us all. He declares that He has come so that all, who were born in sin and struggle through this world of woe, can live an abundant life in Him.

I have never questioned why I faced the anxiety and depression that I have shared with you. Perhaps to you, it gives hope and context to your own situation. I have learned that there is life after the storm. We best remember Noah for his building of the Ark and endurance through the flood but fail to remember that when the rain ceased and the waters receded, Noah lived on. In fact, for another three hundred and fifty years after stepping off the ark onto the mountains of Ararat, Noah lived on! The storm that you face, however fierce or fateful it may seem, isn't the end of your life. It may seem like you will never survive, but you will, and there will be life after the flood. For me, that is what I needed to hear—"Jamin, you'll be okay." That is what I wanted the doctor to tell me on that day in her office. Now I understand that I searched for the right answer in the wrong place. His Word tells me I am an overcomer, and I can triumph in His name. Although referenced earlier in this book, I must point your attention again to Isaiah 59:19—"When the enemy shall come in like a flood, the Spirit of the LORD shall lift up a standard against him." The flood is neither the finale or finishing phase of your life. The Spirit of the Lord will come to your defense, and you, child of God, will live on.

PRACTICAL APPLICATION

I want to share with you the Scriptures that my mom and I prayed that night in her bedroom. There is power in the spoken Word of God. My words might not have any lasting worth, but the Word of God is eternal and shall endure forever. If you take nothing else away from this book, perhaps you can take away these Scriptures to help you combat and overcome the spirit of fear.

I will both lay me down in peace and sleep: for thou, Lord, only maketh me dwell in safety.
Psalm 4:8

The Lord will give strength unto his people; The Lord will bless his people with peace.
Psalm 29:11

Great peace have they which love thy law: and nothing shall offend them.
Psalm 119:165

Peace I leave with you, my peace I give unto you: not as the world giveth, give I unto you. Let not your heart be troubled,

neither let it be afraid.
John 14:27

For God hath not given us the spirit of fear; but of power, and of love, and of a sound mind.
2 Timothy 1:7

And the peace of God, which surpasses all understanding, will guard your hearts and minds through Christ Jesus. Finally, brethren, whatsoever things are true, whatsoever things are honest, whatsoever things are just, whatsoever things are pure, whatsoever things are lovely, whatsoever things are of good report; if there be any virtue, and if there be any praise, think on these things.
Philippians 4:7-8

STILL GONNA PRAISE YOU

The summer had passed and while it was back-to-school season for most, for me it was back to nothing more than the same old thing I had done every day since school let out in May. I was still living out my six month commitment to the Lord and not returning to school was so hard for me to swallow. Although God had delivered me from the attacks of anxiety and depression, I still felt a dull ache and deep loneliness in my heart. I couldn't help but notice everyone else carrying on with their busy lives and chasing their dreams while I was stuck in a northern Minnesota small town. On top of that, I had been hurt and betrayed by a close friend, which left me dealing with a lot of questions about my own self-worth. I began to hear so many rumors about why I hadn't returned to school, and none of them were true. I was too far away to defend myself and to discouraged to hardly care about redeeming myself. I just pulled away. In all reality, friends were what I needed right then, but I shut them out for fear of more hurt and betrayal. The brokenness I experienced was something that took more than a moment to heal. I could have found many reasons to get bitter, but I refused to give the devil that power over me. Nothing and no one is worth allowing bitterness to take root in your heart. Bitterness is more than just a feeling, it is a stronghold that attaches itself to your soul and runs deep. Our relationship with God must be guarded from such a vicious detriment.

I felt completely alone, wondering who I even was anymore. My passion had always been singing, but I wasn't doing that. People had always given me energy, but I had pulled away from my friends because of the hurt. The one thing I felt like I did have going for me was that I had kept my promise to God. As I had committed, I wasn't on any platforms at church, camp, school or anywhere else, yet I felt alone because every comfort zone I'd known was now gone. I knew, at that season of my life, I was in the will of God, but I couldn't understand why I felt like this.

I spent a lot of my free time at the gym working out, and I would often grab coffee from a local shop on my way there. I remember, one day, pulling into the parking lot of the fitness center and just silently sitting there behind the steering wheel with no desire at all to go inside. The coffee was weak and tasteless in my mouth while the loneliness I felt within was wickedly strong. I wondered with numbness what was happening to me. "Who am I anymore," I asked myself. I was, by all accounts, broken. I was broken into pieces. There seemed to be no togetherness or control in my life. Everything was in a mess and seemed so out of my control.

Now I have lived long enough to know that God cannot fix something that isn't broken, but what beauty there is in a broken life restored by the hands of the Master! In the process of God putting us back together, as painful as it may be, there develops a relationship and closeness between you and the Lord like no other. An unbreakable bond is formed through it all which is, perhaps, why God allows us to be broken in the first place. Could it be that His love for the broken is what allows us to be broken? In that brokenness, God pulls us closer to Him than we would have ever pulled ourselves. He works on us, perfecting and purifying that which is already seen as priceless in His eyes. He makes us new and whole, as only He can do. He teaches us through trial and hardship to trust Him. Certainly, we come to see God in a more clear way. Whatever knowledge and understanding we had of Him is expanded and enlarged as we come to see His fullness and grandeur. But the essentiality of all of that taking place is our willingness to allow God to work on us and have His way with our lives. God is able to do a quick work, but not every "fix" is a "quick fix." The world will always offer a quick fix to your life's problems, but its best offers and greatest attempts will leave life's struggles worse off than when they started. We must learn to trust God with our lives and allow Him to grow and develop us even when it takes time.

We live in a disposable generation where broken things are thrown out and replaced by something new and shiny. At best, a broken life is pitied by society today but not much hope or help is extended. God looks upon our brokenness and is moved with compassion.

The sacrifices of God are a broken spirit: a broken and a contrite heart, O God, thou wilt not despise.
Psalm 51:17

Humanity assumes that a pure and holy God would turn away and want nothing to do with a broken heart, yet "the Lord is nigh unto them that are of a broken heart" (Psalm 34:18). He sees us, even then, as all the more beautiful. In time of desperate need, He is faithful and true. His love remains unconditional when my condition is less than ideal. The world may consider one worthless in their broken state, but God brings our greatest worth out of such disarray. Only through Jesus do the broken truly become beautiful.

As I sat in my car, I didn't see anything beautiful. All I could see was my brokenness. No friend or family members words could cheer me up, although I desperately wanted to break free from how I felt. I was miserable and ready to do something about it. I decided to do what I knew to do, what I'd always done; I began to pray a vulnerable and honest prayer. Prayer had been my sustaining strength so many times before; therefore, I knew where to go in that low point of life. I didn't run to drugs, alcohol or a relationship. I ran to Jesus! He was my refuge and I began to pray:

"Okay God, I don't understand what's happening in my life right now. I thought I was doing what you wanted me to do! I came home and am working to save money to return to Bible School. I have given up singing to show you that I will serve you beyond a platform, yet I'm dealing with feelings and emotions that I don't know how to handle. God, I'm broken! I hardly know who I am right now. I'm

trying to figure out my calling, but I can hardly feel you. It seems that everything exciting and happy in my life has come to an end. I feel numb, but God I do still love you. You're still so real to me."

When I got to that place in the prayer, something came over me. It's as if God paralleled this moment with my moment of commitment back at IBC, and that same fervent devotion to God welled up within me. That's when I said it:

"No matter what happens, God, I'm still gonna serve you. I'm still gonna love you. I'm still gonna praise my way through this hard, hard time."

When those words had been spoken and that prayer had been prayed, the presence of the Lord filled my car. I didn't want the moment to end so I turned on some gospel music. My playlist was on shuffle mode, and the first song was chosen at random to begin playing. I listened and was stunned. Israel Houghton was singing what I needed to hear:

"It's not over, it's not finished.
It's not ending, it's only the beginning.
When God is in it, all things are new.
All things are new."

I hadn't heard that song in forever, but it was undeniably for me that day. It had been months since I had heard from God, but I heard Him clearly in that moment. This wasn't the end! It wasn't over for me! God was beginning something new in my life. I, later, stepped out of that car with a new perspective, a new joy, a new peace and a new outlook. I now knew that God was with me and leading me through this for a greater purpose. He was bringing me closer to Him and using my brokenness to bring forth beauty. I knew it was the beginning of something, but I never could have dreamed what that something was. My prayer becoming a song and being recorded on an IBC Live recording, reaching millions around the world? No way. Marrying the love of my life, in a love story better than I could've planned for myself, and singing with him? No way. Getting the opportunity to record a full album of our original songs in Nashville, TN? What a crazy thought! Traveling the country, sharing the truth of Jesus Christ through Word, song and testimony? Nah, that seemed totally unrealistic, yet, in all reality, this was the very "something" God was up to.

I learned that we can never plan, ourselves, what God has already planned for our lives. As the heavens are higher than the earth, so are God's ways higher than our ways, and His thoughts above our thoughts (Isaiah 55:9). He has divine purpose for each of us. The verse in Jeremiah that is so often quoted is true:

For I know the thoughts that I think toward you, saith the LORD, thoughts of peace, and not of evil, to give you an expected end.
Psalm 51:17

Looking at the original language from which that verse was translated, I better understood what the Lord was saying when he spoke of the "expected end" that He would give. According to

Strong's Hebrew Dictionary, one definition for the word "expected" is something one longs for. The word "end" is defined as also meaning future. Could it be that the Lord was saying that His desire is to give us the future that we long for? Of course, God will not grant or give anything that is contrary to His Word and will; however, for those who submit themselves to God and delight themselves in the Lord, "he shall give thee the desires of thine heart" (Psalm 37:4).

Sometimes, when in the heat of the battle, it is easy to consider our stress, fear, and loneliness and see death and defeat as our expected end, but that is not looking through the eyes of faith. If we lift our eyes away from the emotion of our misery and gaze toward His greater purpose for our lives and pursue after that, we will undoubtedly see our own future as God sees it. If we keep the faith and trust only in Him, He will always orchestrate our lives so that every purpose is attained and every promise fulfilled.

> *"'Tis so sweet to trust in Jesus,*
> *Just to take Him at His word;*
> *Just to rest upon His promise;*
> *Just to know, thus saith the Lord.*
> *Jesus, Jesus, how I trust Him,*
> *How I've proved Him o're and o're*
> *Jesus, Jesus, precious Jesus!*
> *O for grace to trust Him more."*

FINDING GOD IN THE STORM

Do you know what I find amazing? The disciples—the men

who forsook all for serving Jesus and witnessed the most magnificent miracles this side of heaven—didn't fully understand who He was until He took them through a storm.

Countless times they had witnessed His power demonstrated first hand. They had watched the grace He dealt and the mercy He multiplied to those so undeserving. They saw the compassion He had toward the broken. They saw Him defy the laws of what they perceived as impossible and, so many times, He did the impossible among them. Yet, on at least two occasions while at sea, those twelve ordinary men were amazed and astounded at His power. When Jesus awoke from His sleeping in the back of the boat, and spoke to the sea saying "... Peace, be still," the disciples "feared exceedingly, and said one to another, What manner of man is this, that even the wind and the sea obey him?" (Mark 4:39-41). Another time when Jesus walked on the water to reach them in their troubled situation, "They that were in the ship came and worshipped him, saying, Of a truth thou art the Son of God" (Matthew 14:33). Perhaps it would've taken me awhile to catch on also, but how many miracles must He per-form in our lives before we open our eyes to the truth of who He is?

His many miracles performed among the multitudes were not enough to convince them of His all sufficient power. They had witnessed Him feed the five thousand, heal the sickened multitudes, raise the dead and forgive the unforgivable, but still they were not convinced. It seems that until God personally and directly expressed His love toward them through divine intervention in their time of trouble, their understanding was clouded. They had seen Him help others, but His helping them made all of the difference in their faith. When God walked on the waters that rose against them, they then truly saw and believed Who He was. When God spoke peace to the sea that they feared would drown them all, their eyes were open to the full wonder of His power.

We call them faithless and ignorant, but we are no different than them. We can witness miracles, signs and wonders and believe in God's ability to do them again, yet limit our own understanding of who He is. Sometimes it takes a storm to get our attention. Moments of desperation are where we come to know Him. Trying times of turmoil are where we come to understand the depth of His love and compassion toward us. Sometimes amid howling wind and a rising tide is where we find our ability to trust Him like never before and see Him like we've never seen Him.

We blame the enemy for our storms when, often times, he has nothing to do with them. It's not always the unleashed fury of an angry devil that brings a storm into our lives. Sometimes God sends us there.

And straightway Jesus constrained his disciples to get into a ship, and to go be-fore him unto the other side, while he sent the multitudes away.
Matthew 14:22

They were in the boat and, ultimately, in the storm as a result of the Master's direction. There was divine reason for bringing them and the storm together. What preaching, teaching and even miracles couldn't convince them of, perhaps, a storm could. So, He sent them out at sea.

For me, it wasn't in Sunday services and special events where my spiritual eyes were opened to the fullness of Who He is. It was in a storm out at sea. Don't misunderstand me, I believe in the power of preaching and thank God for every anointed sermon that has shaped my life. I believe in the power of anointed biblical teaching that gives understanding and imparts revelation to our minds, from the Word of God. Yet, I also believe at the same time, that some things in life cannot truly be learned from a lesson taught or a sermon preached. Some things we can only learn through the lesson of experience. Oh, what an experience it was. I look back on it now and see the hand of God upon me. When I couldn't feel Him, He was there. When I thought He wasn't working, He was. When I couldn't understand my own feelings, He did. Though it all, God was faithful. I can see now that I knew Him better when the storm was over. I found God in the storm of my life and so, dare I say it, thank God for the storm!

BUILDING ALTARS

So much had happened between May and September, yet I didn't return to school until January. In the meantime, I worked. Still fulfilling my commitment, I did not sing but started writing sermons about what God was teaching me. When in times past I would go to the piano and practice new songs, I started praying. In those times spent with the Lord, He revealed things in my life and removed things from my heart that didn't align with His will. We are all familiar with what prayer is but not nearly familiar enough with the practice of prayer. Prayer is that place where God pulls out of us what we can't bring ourselves to pull out. Be it pride, fear, doubt, complacency or hurt, we really can pray our way out of their grip. Fears that I had let haunt me were now brought forth and made visible to me as the lies they really were. Misguided confidence that I had placed in relationships with others was finding its proper place in my relationship with Jesus. The validation that I sought to receive from others, I now found in Him. Although I never struggled with low self-esteem, I had discovered my true identity as a child of God. I thank God for those six months I spent away from the platform, because that season brought revealing and reshaping to the person I really was when the lights were turned off, the microphone put away and the platform was empty.

It all came out as I earnestly prayed and sought the Lord. He worked on me and worked on me. Things that I didn't even know were there, He worked on until they were no more a part of me. No wonder I was broken! Spiritual impurities and poisons were killing me until I surrendered them all into the hands of the one who makes all things new. Jesus asks us as He asked the lame man at Bethesda's pool, "Do you want to be made whole?" Don't look any further or search for another to make sense of your struggle and circumstances. Allow Him to work until His reflection is seen through your life.

Everything in which my identity had always been placed was gone. I had now found my identity in Jesus. Every afternoon I spent in prayer, away from some recreational activity, wasn't in vain; I was building altars. Every late night hour in which I buried hot tears in my pillow was not pointless; I was building altars.

Little did I know then what I would be doing now, evangelizing and traveling from coast to coast with my husband, on more platforms than I could have ever dreamed of. I don't say that, at all, to boast. I am humbled that God has allowed me the privilege to serve and share Him with others; however, before God would allow me this privilege of standing on so many public platforms, I had to build private altars. The notability of the platform you stand on, however big or small, must never replace the necessity of the altar you kneel at. The only way you will ever effectively minister and be, at all, anointed on a platform is by way of brokenness and humbleness at an altar. You can experience His blessing, abide in His grace and adhere to His commandments, yet miss out on the glory of His presence found only at an altar. In the Old Testament Tabernacle, the brazen altar was the first piece of furniture found inside the entrance. Before any other place or piece of furniture could be visited, one must first come to the altar.

The first thing Noah did after emerging from the Ark, following the flood, was build an altar to the Lord. Abram built an altar before laying upon it His own son to be sacrificed. Moses built an altar and named it "The Lord is My Banner". David built an altar on the threshing-floor. Joshua built an altar to the Lord in Mount Ebal. Gideon made an altar to the Lord on top of the rock. These are just a few of the many prominent people in the Old Testament who built altars unto the Lord. I could list many more, but the built altars of others can only affect our lives so much. We must build our own.

If you have never built an altar, or perhaps it has been awhile, I encourage you to find a place to kneel before God and build an altar in your life. Although altars do require sacrifice, it is there where the fire of God falls and consumes what we have offered unto the Lord. The same God of Elijah, Who responded by fire, is still responding to us today. We must have the fire and anointing of His Spirit upon all we do.

My best effort to make a difference on my own will fall short, but if I have built an altar where God's anointing can saturate my life, then much can be accomplished by His Spirit. I have seen first-hand what happens when the anointing takes over in a service: chains fall from marriages fettered by failure, the stronghold of drug and alcohol addictions are broken down, immorality, per-version and homosexuality are overcome by His power, sin in its every form is forgiven by the blood and washed away by bap-tism in Jesus Name, depression and anxiety dissipate in a single moment. Oh, I pray that we all build such altars in our lives that we see those same results on a daily basis, not just on Sunday morning and Wednesday night. May we all strive to live in a dimension of power and authority in the Spirit where we can see God's Word made manifest through us.

> *And these signs shall follow them that believe; In my name shall they cast out devils; they shall speak with new tongues; They shall take up serpents; and if they drink any deadly thing, it shall not hurt them; they shall lay hands on the sick, and they shall recover.*
> *Mark 16:17-18*

How we all desire to be used by God and see those things hap-pen, yet it can not happen without altars. We must possess a re-newed longing to truly know Him, in Whom we have believed; to get to a place—whether by a storm or not—where we live a life overflowing with abundance, blessing and favor. True purpose, real joy and unspeakable peace are found only in the security and safety of a daily altar experience.

The altar keeps you. So, I challenge you to build an altar; in your room, in your car, in your closest. Build altars of sacrifice and devotion to God.

CHAPTER NINE

traveler's guide to happiness

Happy is that people, whose God is the Lord.
Psalm 144:15

The most frequently asked questions I am asked about our life-style and ministry are about traveling. People wonder if I love it or hate it and I must admit, I love it. I wouldn't trade this time of our life for anything. Even living full-time in our RV is exciting. Sometimes I struggle to fathom and remember what it was like to live in house. We love RV living!

While traveling, whether by car, airplane or motorhome, I have discovered a few things along the way that are sure to bring joy and happiness to a traveler's life.

1. THE SINGLE HAPPIEST MOMENT OF A TRIP IS YOUR INITIAL ARRIVAL AT THE DESTINATION.

We are constantly on the move and sometime visit multiple places and cities within a week's time. Churches are so very kind to us, far beyond what we deserve. Pastors and their wives all over this country have believed in us, supported us and blessed us in so many ways. We are forever indebted to the kindness of so many. I can't explain how welcoming it is and how special we feel when we walk into a hotel room, airbnb, evangelist quarters or someone's beautiful home and are surprised by a lovely personalized wel-come basket. I'll never forget flinging open window curtains to see the magical view of the St. Louis Arch, majestic Idaho mountains or a Minnesota lake nestled among tall pines. It's pure joy! I immediately rummage through the basket, sampling the necessities: chocolate, of course. I love to scrapbook our travels, so I make sure to always snap pictures of the coziness of everything we do and everywhere we go. I'm told that I tend to express excitement in the form of a high pitched abbreviated squeal. I think there are a lot of those in our travels. Of course, the excitement wears off a bit after awhile, and we settle ourselves into routines and responsibilities.

One of my daily routines is a time of prayer, reading and writing in my journal. I always make the time to rehearse on paper what I have just realized, learned or understood through prayer or reading. Preserving those moments and thoughts, and making them available for later reflection, is so special to me because, page by page, I realize that they never die.

Walking has also become one of my favorite pass times. Sometimes outside and sometimes inside to a workout video; I make sure that I am doing everything I can to counter balance my love and consumption for chocolate. Oh, how I love dark chocolate. There is a bar in my purse at all times!

No matter how splendorous or simple a place may be, I have learned this obvious, yet revelatory, truth: We bring ourselves with us wherever we go. Our hearts, habits, routines, passions and problems—they all come along with us. Fears, faith, forgiveness and forebodings aren't tucked away and pulled out only on special occasions. We may try to suppress them and slip away for a night out, free from them, but they go with you. Even when unexpressed and lying quiet, they are there. They all come along for the ride with us. The scientifically supported faction of excitement—that rush of adenine that gives a burst of energy—may indeed distract us from the baggage we bear, but it does not take them off our hands. Whatever the contents, good or bad, the bags are ours and they come to.

2. SHORT TRIPS PROVIDE HAPPINESS AS WELL AS THE LONG ONES.

Sometimes Jeremy and I are only in one place for a couple of days or, while traveling through an area, we may only have a few hours to spare, but it is amazing how much fun you can fit into a short amount of time.

When I realized that Jeremy and I were passing through Paris, TX one Saturday afternoon, I insisted we stop for a romantic photo opt at their Texas style replica of the Eiffel Tower, complete with a red cowboy hat on top. I know it's not a two week vacation in the far reaches of the world, but those fun little moments make life special. We may only spend five minutes at a historical landmark or sight of interest, but it's long enough to show my scrapbook we've been there. Take a seat in our RV living room and I'll show you photos of some of our favorite memories from spontaneous moments of travel:

- Spray painting our names on the cars at Cadillac Ranch in Amarillo, TX.
- Posing in our church clothes in front of the iconic blue whale that sits perched in a Catoosa, Oklahoma pond.
- Roaming the highways of northern Idaho and western Montana with no planned route or destination.
- Hiking three miles along an Arkansas mountain bluff to see a picturesque cliff that we never did find.
- Taking the long route back to Boise just so I could say I've been

to Washington state.

- The time I was given a two-hour notice to pack my bags and prepare for a train ride into downtown Chicago where would spend the night and next day exploring the Magnificent Mile.
- Walking the muddy Oregon Trail in Baker City, Oregon to see the wagon ruts in the ground.
- Ducking into the Memphis Peabody Hotel to watch the ducks walk the red carpet. The memory was topped off by eating a white chocolate duck filled with ganache, and a coffee-cup shaped tiramisu desert.
- Picnicking on a river bank in the middle of the Idaho mountains.
- Going on an official coffee tour through Huntsville, Alabama and getting my "coffee passport" stamped at every location.
- Eating the world's largest ding-dong at a Texas antique mall with a pastor and his wife on our way out of town, after preaching for them.

Happy is he that hath the God of Jacob for his help, whose hope is in the Lord his God:
Psalm 146:5

3. MAKE MEMORIES THAT LAST WHEN THE TRIP IS OVER.

Oh, the memories we have made together. We have embarked upon twenty-four hour camping trips that have provided endless memories and laughing. On one of our camping excursions, we whipped the car around at eight in the morning and paused the trip to check out a bakery whose claim to excellence was their supposed world famous recipes, only to eat what was the worst coconut cream pie ever made. On the same trip, while camping in a crowded lake-side campground, our car alarm was set off at two o'clock in the morning, and the air went out of the mattress. You can laugh about those memories, but you can't make them up.

We also have made countless memories with pastors' families and friends from all across the country. Truly, during our evangelistic travels, we have made life-long friends that we deeply cherish. We have had impromptu baseball games with preacher's kids in the back field behind the church and eaten like cajuns at crawfish boils in their back yards. From horseback riding through tall thorn bushes to spilling coffee on a pastor's wife's beautiful champagne colored blazer, we are sure to make memories, intentionally or not, that last forever.

STATES AND STORIES

Traveling can be exhausting. No matter what conveniences you have or how long you've done it, it's exhausting. We are very careful to consider that and try to make sure that we always prioritize our ministry opportunities above and before any pleasurable activity that would cause us to be less than ready to minister at our best. There are times that we fly or drive into a city and, exhausted from a day of travel, must go straight into service. I've often wondered where we would get the strength to give it our all, yet, when service starts, God supernaturally carries us to a place of strength that we were too weak to attain ourselves. As the presence of God moves and I see hungry saints, first time visitors and broken back-sliders being changed by the power of God, every ounce of exhaustion seems to leave. That is what it's all about!

Those moments keep us humble. In our weak and exhausted state we are reminded that it is not our strength that heals, delivers or saves, it is the power of the almighty God. He alone is mighty to save. We do not travel this beautiful country just to see the sights, entertain churches, sing our songs or preach feel-good sermons that leave people unchanged. We do it for the glory of God and the furtherance of His Kingdom. One soul repenting of their sin, being baptized in His Name and being filled with His Spirit is worth the investment of our lives.

I love to see God do what only He can do. I'm amazed at the power of His presence to bring couples together. Over and over I have watched a visiting husband slip his arm around his wife while, together, they overwhelmingly feel the warm and peaceful presence of God for the first time. I love to see healing sweep across a congregation and, in response, see people reach out and touch the hem of His garment. I love to see addicts delivered and the broken put back together. That is what I live for! Those things, and many more, are the reasons I will gladly beat the roads and give all of my energy, effort and ability to spreading this glorious truth. If our blessed lives can be a blessing to someone else, it is worth it all.

Pack your bags and come on the road with us as I reminisce on some of the stories that have unfolded in our travels from state to state.

MISSOURI

Jeremy and I had only been married a few months, and I was still settling into life as an evangelist's wife when our travels took us to Missouri. We were ministering at a church and, during the altar service, I noticed a woman in the back weeping. I felt led to go talk with her, so I made my way to her row. After introducing myself, I asked if there was anything I could pray with her about. Sobbing and visibly moved by my concern, she said "My daughter, pray for my daughter. Her counselors say there is nothing more they can do for her. She will not open up to me or anyone else." She stopped, long enough to take a deep heavy breath, and then looked at me straight in the eyes, "I just want her to be saved."

Wow! Isn't that the prayer of every parent? This beautiful woman had just found truth and was allowing God to transform her life. She had been, for so long, trapped in a world of drug addiction and alcohol consumption until finding this precious church that had taught her truth and exposed her to the saving and delivering power of God. Now all she desired was for her daughter to find the same freedom and deliverance that she herself had found. We prayed that God would intervene in her daughter's life and help her to leave behind the addictions, parties and unfulfilled relationships and come to find her true purpose and joy in Jesus. I held her and we cried together. I had never met this woman prior to the moment before, however, I was shaken and so deeply moved by her story.

It was, for me, a reality reminder of just how deadly the world's devices are and how desperately people are desiring to be set free. While the world screams that they should just take another hit, turn up another bottle and party another night, their own soul is screaming out for help. They feel fixed in this tug of war within themselves. I believe in counseling and professional help, but sometimes the issues of our day are beyond anything a counselor can counsel you through. Our world needs the power of God. Jesus is the only escape from a life of sin. Obedience to Peter's message, recorded in Acts 2:38, is God's only plan of true salvation, and the world needs to hear it! I became so burdened that day, not only for this woman and her daughter but for the world around us that is lost. I was convicted to take up more responsibility to share this glorious, soul-saving message everywhere that I go. Every unsatisfied sinner may feel hopeless, but we know where their hope is. Hope is in Jesus!

MISSISSIPPI

While people flooded the altars at the close of service and were responding to the power of God, a little nine year old bus girl also made her way to the front and, almost unnoticed by most, stood behind a group of praying ladies and lifted up her hand. It was obvious that this was new to her. She hardly knew what to do, yet she knew she wanted to feel what everyone else was feeling and experiencing. She knew this was real. I walked over and encouraged her to just talk to Jesus. Very timidly she began to talk to Jesus as she would a friend. Tears flowed down her cheeks. The church people gathered around, moved by her sensitivity to God's Spirit.

Later in the service, the pastor called her up to the platform and told her story. She had recently started riding the church bus to Sunday morning services and had told the driver that her mom and two other adults in her life had told her that the world would be better off without her. Can you believe that? I couldn't. What mother, or any other person for that matter, would tell a darling child to commit suicide? I cannot fathom that. Unfortunately, this is the world we live in. I thank God for the saint of God who climbs behind the wheel of that church van and weekly gives that girl an escape, if only for a few hours, from the hopeless environment she did not choose. I honor every bus driver, Sunday school teacher, ministry leader and church volunteer that selflessly give of themselves to make a difference in someones life.

As she stood there on that platform, tears flowing from her eyes, I reached up and took her hand. That precious church stretched forth their hands and began to pray for her as she again, with hands lifted, responded to the presence of God she felt. I told her how much Jesus loved her and has plans for her life. "In fact," I said, "He died so that you could live!" As she repented of her sin and began worshiping to the Lord, that closed-off and broken little girl began to leap for joy. There's no telling how long it had been since she'd known much joy, yet here in the presence of God she couldn't help but rejoice. I walked with her off the platform and danced in the altar with her. In a matter of moments, God filled her with the gift of the Holy Ghost, with the evidence of speaking in other tongues! That is the love, grace and power of our God.

These are the moments that leave me at a loss for words by their divine beauty. Jeremy and I love the benefits of traveling and seeing this great country we call home, but we are not tourists. We are motivated to pack up the RV and move on to the next church because we whole-heartedly believe that what God did for this precious nine year old, God will do for whosoever will believe and obey.

ARKANSAS

We love Arkansas. Jeremy preached there a lot before we got

married and made so many friends that I now cherish also. In a Sunday morning service, following a full weekend of revival, a first-time visitor walked in. She was a beautiful girl in her senior year of high school and I remember noticing how striking she looked. So much so that some might be intimidated by her beauty. During the service, she seemed unmoved and unemotional as she sat in her pew. My curious self wondered what she thought of everything. Isn't it funny how we look at someone so young and beautiful and assume that they have it all together, that they aren't searching for something?

At the end of that service, that young lady began to respond to the presence of the Lord and was filled with the gift of the Holy Ghost. She had been so emotionless and reserved but, when she finished praying, was adorned with the most beautiful smile and glow of joy. The pastor explained what she had experienced and pointed out her need, based upon Scripture, to be baptized in Jesus Name. She understood it and said she would ask her parents that afternoon if she could be baptized that night in the evening service. Her parents were reluctant and suggested she wait and be baptized at their church in the titles of Father, Son and Holy Ghost. Although she had not sat through weeks of Bible Study and heard months of apostolic teaching and preaching, she was persistent and determined to be baptized in Jesus Name. She had quickly, that morning, received the revelation that only the Name could wash sin away. Her parents permitted and even came that night to see her buried in the waters of baptism and take on the Name of Jesus.

While my husband was preaching that night, a group of visitors walked in. No one knew them or had invited them, yet how exciting! I think Jeremy was actually beginning to close his message but, when they walked in, preached on awhile longer. When the altar call was given, one of the men came to the altar and earnestly prayed and repented. When the pastor announced that this young lady and another new convert would be baptized, He asked if there was anyone else who wanted to be baptized in Jesus Name. Immediately that visitor, who had come late and prayed in the altar, raised his hand! That night, three were baptized in Jesus Name.

After the service was dismissed, that man told us his story. He'd prayed earlier that day and asked the Lord to lead him to the church where He needed to be baptized. Again, no one had invited him or even told him about this church. The Lord quite literally led him to the only church in town that preached the message of Jesus Name baptism. God had so beautifully orchestrated that service to be one focused on baptism. How incredible God is! To see the gradual, yet distinct transformation of a soul who has repented, been baptized in Jesus Name and filled with the Holy Ghost is a beautiful thing. The closest thrill that even comes close to the glory of your own salvation experience is to witness someone else receive the same experience, and that never gets old.

Another special memory we have in Arkansas is our first Valentine's Day as a married couple. It fell on a Wednesday night that year and we were scheduled to minister at a church that evening in Camden, Arkansas. To make the occasion as special as possible, we celebrated a night early. Jeremy took me to an Italian restaurant in a nearby bigger city, and we had a lovely evening together. The pastor we were preaching for that next evening had informed Jeremy that he wasn't able to be there; however, he had made dinner reservations for the two of us immediately following service at a delicious local restaurant, Post Master's Grill. It was an old historic post office building that had been creatively converted into a restaurant. Walking up the huge concrete steps and through the vintage wooden front door was like stepping back in time. Post Office boxes still covered the wall behind the hostess stand. We were blown away! This small Arkansas town has a real gem.

We gave them our names and were led to the back dining room. Their dinner rush had been earlier in the evening, and being that it was around nine o'clock, we were the only ones in the restaurant. The atmosphere was incredibly romantic, complete with candlelight and a red rose on the table. We enjoyed the most delicious four course meal, served and presented so elegantly. Somehow it was even more special than anything we could have planned for ourselves, because it was thoughtfully gifted to us so unexpectedly. Again, I was still new and adjusting to marriage and life as an evangelist's wife, yet this made me realize that God takes care of us. Far beyond just our basic needs, He is so faithful to extend undeserved favor and, through precious people, provide sweet memories that last a lifetime. Truly, the moments that I hold most dear are not those spent in the limelight, instead they are those quiet, divinely orchestrated God moments.

During that same time period, while in Arkansas, we spent a week in an evangelist quarters. It was a Monday evening and we were having prayer time. Kneeling at opposite ends of a long couch, we sought the Lord and He heard us. After some time, I looked up and actually noticed, as if I was looking at a picture after the fact, that we were doing what I'd always dreamed of doing with my husband. As I saw us both kneeling together in prayer, my mind transported me back to my IBC dorm room where at my own couch, a couple of years earlier, I had asked the Lord to send me a man who would kneel next to me and pray. And there we were. God had already given Jeremy and myself so many confirmations, prior to our engagement, that we were meant to be together, but never was a moment more beautiful than when I realized that this prayer from my past had been answered. God truly has given me the desires of my heart.

OKLAHOMA

It was a Sunday night service, and a visitor walked in late, just after worship service had begun. She sat through the service intently listening and taking it all in. Throughout the preaching of the Word of the Lord, she became visibly moved by the tangible presence of God. Tears rolled down her cheeks. Having never experienced anything like this, she couldn't stop crying and shaking. In the altar, she apologized to us for her uncontrollable behavior. We, of course, smiled and explained to her that an apology was not necessary. She was feeling the presence of God! She prayed and, although not receiving the Holy Ghost that night, was overcome with a contagious smile and sense of joy.

After the service was dismissed she told the pastor's wife that she had planned to commit suicide that evening but, after being invited to that evening's service by a church member, decided to attend the service and would proceed with her plans afterward. Of course, we knew that her attendance that night wasn't an accident or coincidence. After feeling and experiencing the power of God, she, too, understood how divine this encounter was. Hours earlier she had not desired to live but, after feeling the presence of God and hearing the hope found in His Word, she possessed a new desire.

That is exactly why our churches must have both spirit and truth. We have no idea who will walk in, what they are fighting and how their past encounters with religion have left them all the more hopeless. They need to feel the genuine power of God and experience real change in their lives. We cannot afford to go through the motions and take one service, or the moving of His Spirit, for granted. We must praise Him with an intentional desire to see His glory come down. The Bible clearly states in Psalm 22:3 that the Lord "inhabits the praises of Israel"; therefore, we must worship and praise Him until He settles down into our midst. If not only for yourself, do it with the understanding that some broken, desperate, suicidal individual is depending on your praise to usher them into His presence.

On a much lighter note, I remember another Oklahoma evening where I was asked to preach! We sang a few songs and then Jeremy and I traded our normal places; he went to the piano, and I stepped to the pulpit. I had prayed, prepared and studied what the Lord had given me to share. I was both nervous and excited. After reading through my notes and rehearsing, I realized that the message would nearly take forty minutes to deliver. I had never preached that long! I usually did good to make it across the twenty-five minute mark, but I guess I had a lot to say this time. That night while preaching, about two thirds of the way through the sermon, I humorously noticed one woman sleeping, another clipping her finger nails and a visitor who put on make-up, twice! My message, obviously, wasn't as good as I had hoped it would be. My husband and I laughed and laughed about it after service. God moved mightily in several lives that night, but if I never preach forty minutes again, you will know why!

MINNESOTA

I grew up calling this northern wonderland of adventure home. I suppose that explains my loves for moose, cozy cabins, any sport involving snow or a motor and all things northern. The prominent coffee shop in Minnesota is called Caribou Coffee. It's marketing portrays Minnesotan culture and life. Nearly every store is decorated to look like some hunting cabin or ski resort lodge. My favorite place to sit is next to the fireplace with my feet propped up on a tree stump stool. Oh, and I must mention that what sets them apart is the real chocolate chips that they melt down and put into their mochas. It is a million times better than the bottled chocolate sauce that many shops use. It is the most delicious mocha. For me, it is a taste of home and brings back so many happy memories each time I take a sip.

While preaching around Minnesota one summer and spending an afternoon at Caribou studying, I spotted an adorable set of new mugs that they were selling. One in particular caught my eye and I squealed over its cuteness. I told Jeremy how much I wanted it but, in all reality, I knew it was silly to buy another mug. We have so many mugs already that, as Jeremy says, we rattle down the road. Two days later, we walked into the wonderful church in Andover, Minnesota and was handed a gift basket. I almost fell over. How did they know? Who told them? That very mug that I had so desperately wanted, along with a Caribou gift card and bag of chocolate covered espresso beans was in that basket! I was amazed. It may sound piddly to you, but you cannot tell me that Jesus does not care about even the little things that we care about. Believe it or not, I think Jeremy may use that mug even more than I do!

As miraculous as I thought that was, we've seen greater miracles. One occurred as the result of a Minnesota youth rally. A sixteen year old young man stood in front of peers and leaders to share some devastating news. A recent MRI had led to his diagnosis of hydrocephalus, which is the medical term for water being on one's brain. With much emotion, he proclaimed with great faith, "I know God will heal me." I was at the piano sobbing my eyes out and confidently believing in my heart, as did he, that God would heal him. Not a week later, we received news that another MRI had been done and the doctors were amazed to report that there was absolutely no water on his brain. Call it what you want, but I call it a miracle! Miracles still happen and God still honors faith.

IDAHO

In this nearly forgotten northwestern state there is much more than just potatoes, as one might assume. Idaho is the most beautiful place I've ever visited. Snow capped mountain peaks are everywhere and from atop one, looking down on the others, you realize just how amazing the creative power of our God is. I remember waking up early on a Saturday morning and, after stopping for coffee, taking off for a day of driving down the scenic highways that weave through mountain passes and even gravel logging roads that wind up the side of the peaks. While sometimes the sheer height can get your heart rate up, the beauty is just as exhilarating. Driving these roads, Jeremy introduced me to a country gospel song that put the whole day into perspective. When his little girl asked him what God looked like, Marty Raybon sang:

"Baby I don't know, but I can tell you this.
I've been to the ocean, I've stood on a mountain
I've seen a sunset burn away a sky of blue
I've stared up at the starlight, got lost in the midnight
I've never seen the face of God,
But I've seen what He can do"

While the majestic mountains and beautiful scenery were unlike anything I'd ever seen, that wasn't at all the extent of what God had done in Idaho.

On the last night of a week-long revival, several people were miraculously healed, including myself. One man told us the next morning that the pain in his leg, that he'd dealt with for several years, was totally gone. In another revival, one lady testified of severe neck pain leaving her body in an instant. Those skeptics that say God is no longer able to perform that same miracles of which we read about in Scripture have obviously not given God a chance. He is still the same yesterday, today and forever. For those that have faith and believe, God is still demonstrating His power with miracles, signs and wonders!

TEXAS

One of our favorite subjects of conversation, when visiting with fellow evangelists or pastors who once evangelized, is the hilarious things that tend to occasionally happen while traveling. A go-to story of my own occurred at a precious country church in Texas. It was Sunday morning and I'd just stepped out of the shower when I realized that my blow dryer and curling iron didn't get packed into my suitcase. This had never happened before. I didn't know what to do! We were twenty minutes from the nearest store and had to be at the church to sound-check in exactly thirty minutes from this horrific moment that ruined my morning. There was nothing else to do but throw my wet soggy hair up into an old fashioned granny bun. I did my best to pull it off, but there was no hope. Thankfully, the moving of God's Spirit isn't predicated on our appearance. We had a wonderful service that morning, but I was determined to find a curling iron before the evening service. While in town for lunch, we stopped at Walmart and purchased what I needed to bail myself out of a bad hair day. An afternoon nap helped me to feel and look rested, but the real progress took place when I plugged the curling iron in. I curled every strand of hair on my head. I had more curls than I knew what to do with. To say the least, I felt like a different women compared to the one I looked like that morning.

We arrived at the church that evening and, following pre-service prayer, we sat on the front bench waiting for the service to begin. A friend of my husbands was there that night and sat down with us to talk for moment. While we are all talking, an elderly gentlemen who we'd met that morning came up and started talking with us. After a few moments he stopped and with a puzzled look on his face, asked me while pointing to Jeremy's friend, "Are you his wife?" I said, "No, I'm Jeremy's wife!" He was shocked and with a dumbfounded stare said to Jeremy, "You mean to tell me she is the same women that was here with you this morning?" I knew I looked bad, but apparently I looked worse than I thought I did!

OHIO

The first time we preached in Ohio, we took our RV and evangelized around the state for a few weeks. We parked the RV at a campground for most of that time and traveled out in our car to where we were preaching on the weekends. After one extended weekend trip, being gone five days, we decided to load up on groceries before arriving at the RV. And I do mean load up. We spent nearly $200, which may not be a lot for some but, considering that we live in an RV and don't have as much space as a home kitchen or residential fridge might have, it was a lot for us. I was so excited to try some new Pinterest recipes since we were going to be in the RV for the following few weeks.

When we pulled into the campground, I was focused on getting the groceries inside, but Jeremy quickly became focused on something else. He immediately noticed before ever walking inside that neither of our air conditioners were running. It was over ninety degrees outside that day and when I climbed the steps inside the RV with my first handful of grocery bags, I realized that it was ninety-nine degrees inside! I was in shock. Everything was off: the air, the refrigerator, the lights. Nothing worked. I didn't understand it all but after a few minutes Jeremy explained that the fuse box on the campground power pole, that we were plugged into, had blown. Somewhere over the course of our five days away, probably not long after we left, all power to our motorhome was lost and everything in the RV that required electricity had stopped working, including the refrigerator. All the groceries in our refrigerator and freezer were ruined and there I was with all my new groceries yet nowhere cool to put them.

The good news was that there was another 50 amp power plug at the camping site next to us, which was empty. Jeremy plugged our cord in and, thankfully, everything came back on without any issues or anything being damaged. We threw away what was ruined and tried to salvage as much of the new groceries as we could. While the fridge was now running and the air conditioner was now blowing, it was going to take a good long while for both of them to cool down. Again, it was over 90 degrees outside with high humidity, and there was no way we could sit in that hot RV. What were we going to to?

There wasn't much we could do except make the best of it. We jumped in the car and figured that the best way for us to cool down was to grab ice cream from a charming local soda fountain. We had seen a lake close by, so we found ourselves a picnic bench by the water where we could eat our ice cream cones in the shade and watch sailboats cruise past. It ended up being a hilarious and fun memory as we couldn't help but laugh about how unexpected life can be.

WISCONSIN

We haven't preached much in Wisconsin but have often traveled through. I used to beat those roads while driving home from

IBC on breaks and back to school when the break was over. Jeremy and I were traveling through Wisconsin one time on our way to Indiana and I couldn't help but request we take exit 116 off of interstate 94. There were two giant orange moose statues, one majestically standing next to a small lake, that I always thought were adorable. When we took that exit and the moose came into view, I squealed in excitement. We parked the RV, bought some incredible fresh squeaky cheese curds and took our pictures for the scrapbook. It was a quick stop, but my heart was full for the remainder of the trip.

PENNSLYVANIA

Perhaps as far as sight seeing goes, one of my all-time favorite days was the day we woke up early and drove to Hershey, Pennsylvania. We have yet to see much of this beautiful state, but our drive that morning was stunning. We sipped on coffee and listened to old music from Jeremy's southern gospel collection and then arrived at Hershey World. I had been there once before but wanted to experience it with Jeremy. My love for chocolate was unrestrained that day and pretty much any other day for that matter. Jeremy told me I was acting like a kid in a candy factory. How could I not?!

We made many memories that day. We participated in a chocolate taste testing activity and saw every step of how chocolate is made. Perhaps the most memorable part of our trip was making our own candy bars and cruising down chocolate avenue. It was fun and special and those are usually the most beautiful memories. Six hours in a magical chocolate world was more than enough for this chocolate lover to have a spectacular day.

LOUISIANA

Louisiana is a long way from Minnesota, but I've fallen in love with cajun food. I never knew how wonderful and full of flavor it was! I must admit that it took me a while to get comfortable peeling boiled crawfish. I used to cringe and nearly gag when someone mentioned the word, but now I can peal and eat them all by myself. I still make plenty of faces and dramatic expressions, from what I am told, but it is an experience everyone should have. One of the first times I tried them was in a crowded restaurant. Jeremy and I were with a few friends, and I was trying my best to build up enough courage to twist off the tail. That's where I struggle. As if the little eyes staring up at me and long antennae curling over aren't heart-attack material enough, the cracking sound of their body being ripped apart is just hard for me to hear. Nevertheless, I was almost to the point of removing the tail when Jeremy scooted back in his chair on the concrete floor, which made the loudest and highest pitched squealing sound. It was worse than nails on a chalkboard, and it scared me to death! I somehow thought it was the crawfish coming to life and instinctively screamed, throwing that poor little crawfish up in the air and onto the floor. It took me awhile to recover, especially from the whole restaurant staring, but I managed.

On our second Valentine's Day as a married couple, we happened to be traveling through Baton Rouge, Louisiana, and spent the evening there. Jeremy introduced me to a beignet shop that is iconic to that area. My life was changed when the first bite melted in my mouth. I became the biggest beignet fan that night.

Several months later, we were traveling through Louisiana

in the RV. We had just closed a revival in Texas and was to begin another in southern Mississippi that coming weekend. Jeremy had driven all afternoon and evening and by midnight was too sleepy to drive any further. He pulled into a Walmart parking lot for the night, where we would sleep until morning. That's right, no hotel room needed, I take my own bed with me to the Walmart parking lot! If you don't know, this is called "dry camping" or "boon-docking" in the RV world, which means that you are not hooked up to water, sewer or electric and depend upon your onboard tanks and generator.

I was relaxing in the bedroom with a book and was clueless concerning where we were or where we had stopped. Jeremy pulled me out of bed and opened up the window shade for me to see what was across the parking lot. It was the same beignet shop we'd been to on Valentines Day! At 12:30 am, we walked into Coffee Call and covered our faces in powdered sugar and carbs with no shame or regret. You can't plan spontaneous memories, and I am convinced they are the best kind.

WHAT MAKES IT WORTH IT?

I love every part of traveling. Life in the RV is something I wouldn't trade for anything. There's nothing like waking up early to hook up the car, bring up the jacks, run in the slides, make fresh coffee and even sometimes grab a Chocolate glazed Cronut if the donut shop parking lot is big enough for us to fit our motorhome in. The excitement of going, doing and moving to the next city for revival services makes me smile big.

I love staring out the big RV window while Jeremy drives, announcing when anything halfway interesting flies by: a cow, a funny sign or a pretty site. I gasp and tell him to look when the sky or horizon is stunningly gorgeous, and I also frequently remind him how boring the mid-western corn fields are for miles and miles and miles. If there's a coffee or donut shop I will, undoubtedly, call for a bathroom break. Jeremy has nearly worked miracles getting that giant RV into tiny parking lots just so I could get my sweet treat fix along the way.

We love stopping at historical centers, museums and tourist sites of all kinds; however, it isn't these places and landmarks that give us joy, purpose and fulfillment. As you have read, we have our share of fun along the way but our real sense of satisfaction comes from seeing the awesome power of God at work everywhere we go.

Ask me about some national park or historical landmark and we may or may not have been there, but ask me about what God is doing in churches, families and individual lives and I'll tell you story after story. Sick bodies are still being healed. Broken lives are still being put back together. Repentant hearts are still finding forgiveness in the blood of Jesus Christ. Sin is still being washed away by baptism in the Name of Jesus. Thousands of people all over the world are being filled with the gift of the Holy Ghost, with the evidence of speaking in other tongues, just like it happened on the day of Pentecost. The Apostles doctrine is still being preached. The Name of Jesus is still the only saving name under heaven. Miracles are still happening. God's Word is still being confirmed with signs following. Alcoholics and drug addicts are still being delivered. Prayer rooms are still being filled. Young people are still pursuing and passionate about the things of God. Elders are still being faithful. Parents are still teaching truth to their children. Husbands and wives are still putting God at the center of their marriages. Sons and daughters who once turned away from God are still being restored. God's voice is still speaking, His Spirit is still moving and His Gospel is still being proclaimed amid this dark and disparaging day. That is what makes this traveler happy.

All of the souvenir shops sell T-shirts and hoodies that say "Not all who wander are lost," but if we wander without a purpose, we are lost. Jeremy and I have committed our lives, not to merely travel or wander the countryside, but to pursue the purpose of God and see His Kingdom come to pass in these last days.

And there are also many other things which Jesus did, the which, if they should be written every one, I suppose that even the world itself could not contain the books that should be written. Amen.
John 21:25

From state to state, as you have read, we have seen God do miraculous things. What Jesus did during His three years of earthly ministry, accounted for in the Gospels, He is still doing today. What the apostles saw in the book of Acts and wrote about in their epistles, we are still seeing on a constant basis. I try my best to journal our lives because I don't want to forget a single thing. I wish I could share with you every story of uncompromised faith and resilient reverence that I've heard and seen. To document every heart touched, every life changed and every soul saved is truly an unattainable goal. I stand with John and concur that, even in my lifetime, the world itself would not be large enough to contain the written wonders and miracles that God has done. That thought alone makes this traveler happy.

———

CHAPTER TEN

*give
me this
mountain*

We were preaching fourteen services in twenty-one days, which meant that there were free days sporadically mixed throughout the trip for us to go sight seeing around the beautiful state of Idaho. As I mentioned in the previous chapter, I had never seen such beautiful scenery. The snow capped mountains of Sun Valley, home to America's very first ski resort, and the winding drive up to the gorgeous mountainous lake town of McCall was unlike any other place I've been. It was so enjoyable to be there and soak in the sights, yet I was dealing with physical pain for most of the trip.

I briefly mentioned, in an earlier chapter, the injury to my back and neck that I suffered while Jeremy and I were dating. It wasn't constant pain or something I even dealt with every day, however, there were frequent flare ups, sometimes lasting for several days, that would effect my strength and stamina while traveling. Muscle spasms in my neck caused me to lie awake through many sleepless nights. I would sometimes in tears have to wake Jeremy up, because the muscle relaxers just didn't touch the pain. We discovered that what helped the most was massage therapy and my husband was so kind to chase down the best place we could find wherever we were.

Almost instantaneous, my neck flared up when we arrived in Idaho. At first, I was too distracted by this new state that I had not been to and it's scenery that I didn't let it affect me, not to mention that Jeremy made our sight seeing days so special. He had been there many times and even spent several months there while we were dating. He took me to the very places that I remembered seeing pictures of, and we took pictures together. After several days of intensifying tightness and pain, I really needed to find a massage therapist. Toward the end of the trip, I broke down and paid for two hour-long overpriced deep tissue massages, without feeling much improvement. Every day I did exercises in the hotel room, but nothing seemed to help. I decided that even with the discomfort and pain, I was going to enjoy every day of being in Idaho and give every service everything I had.

On our very last Sunday of the trip, before flying back to Texas where the RV was parked, I had an experience that changed everything. We were staying in the home of the pastor and his wife that we were preaching for that week. The mother church had a morning and evening service, but Jeremy was also asked to preach an afternoon service at their daughter work in a neighboring community. After lunch, I went back to the house to take a nap, glossy eyed from exhaustion, while Jeremy went to preach. I sat my alarm and was looking forward to feeling rested for the evening service. During my afternoon nap, I had a dream.

I dreamt I was in a two story house surrounded by loved ones. I had lost something, however, and set out to find it upstairs. Once upstairs, in a certain room, I felt a sudden rush of anxiety and fear come over me. I looked around in an attempt to see or figure out what I was feeling, but the room was full of this dark depressing presence. Knowing that I had to immediately get back downstairs where it was peaceful, I raced through the doorway toward the downward staircase. While escaping the room, I felt something pulling at me. I looked back over my shoulder just long enough to see a man in this fear-filled room. He was standing at the door trying to pull me back into the room, but he couldn't quite get a hold of me as I jerked away and ran down the stairs. Startled, that's when I awoke from the dream. Not totally understanding what it all meant, I immediately began to rebuke fear and plead the blood of Jesus. Jeremy soon arrived and we, together, got ready for the evening service. Believe it or not, I did not give the dream another thought until later that evening.

For several days leading up to this Sunday night service I had felt led of the Lord to testify of God's healing power in my life and sing "*My Healer*." While praying in the prayer room before service, I began asking God to heal in that service just as He had so many times healed me. In response to my prayer the Lord said, "I want to heal them, but they must allow me to heal them." With that word from the Lord deposited into my spirit, I knew that if the faith of the people could be built up enough to truly believe on Him for healing, anything could happen!

The service started and the Spirit of the Lord began moving all throughout the worship service. Just before introducing Jeremy and myself to sing and preach, the pastor did something that he had not done all week long. He asked some of the saints to stand and share a testimony of what God had done in their lives. I could hardly believe it! Stories like that are the very thing that build faith in a service. The first one stood and began sharing their story when it hit me. I felt tremendous fear and anxiety hit me like a ton of bricks and race through my body. I had not felt anxiety in years, not since God had delivered me that night in my mom's bedroom. On top of that, I noticed that there was a strange burning sensation in my neck where there was usually pain. My heart was racing and my breath heavy. I was scared. From the front row where I sat, I desperately looked at Jeremy on the platform and motioned for him to come to me. I mouthed the words, "I'm scared." He could not have looked more confused. People were testifying and we were about to minister, yet so much is happening.

In desperation, I grabbed my phone and texted him what I was feeling. Right where he sat on the platform he immediately began to pray, as I slipped out of the service and into the prayer room. Trying to get a good deep breath, I prayed, "If this is an attack of the enemy, I bind him in Jesus name. Devil, I rebuke you and you must flee in the Name of Jesus." As soon as I stepped out of the ser-vice—which robbed Satan of the opportunity to make a scene—and took authority over his attack, my heart rate immediately regulated and the anxious fear I had felt lifted. I walked back to my place on the front pew more sure than ever that I had to share my testimony. The enemy was using fear and anxiety in an attempt to keep me from sharing with those precious people what God wanted to do in that service.

Jeremy looked at me and mouthed, "You need to testify." I nodded in agreement, confident in what I was to do, but so caught up in the moment that I couldn't yet see the whole picture. Just before the pastor handed Jeremy the mic, he made a statement that sealed our confidence in what God was about to do.

"The power of a testimony is that it has the awesome power of building up someone else's faith to believe God for healing in their life."

With that he then said, "Brother and Sister Hart, come and minister." Jeremy made just a few brief remarks and, without any songs, asked me to testify. If I have ever felt the tangible anointing of the Holy Ghost, I felt it that night as the Spirit of God spoke through me to that congregation. I hardly remember all that I said, except that I shared my testimony of God's healing power and declared in faith that God was able to do the miraculous in that very service.

As I began to sing and declare the healing power of God, His undeniable power swept over that sanctuary. From the platform to the back wall, His presence was present to heal. People began flooding the altars, in response to the Spirit of the Lord, before I finished the song. When the song concluded, Jeremy began to exhort and encourage faith for healing and miracles while I went to the piano. Sitting on that bench watching people respond to God's glory and receive healing, I sobbed in awe of His goodness. Again, just like in the prayer room, I heard the voice of the Lord speak in my Spirit: "What the enemy meant for evil, I meant for good."

... ye thought evil against me, but God meant it unto Good, to bring it to pass, as it is this day, to save much people alive.
Genesis 50:20

Suddenly I remembered my dream. It all made perfect sense

now as I looked at the big picture. The enemy wanted to pull me into a dark prison of anxiety and fear so that God's will would be hindered from happening in that service, yet I was safe in the power and authority of the Name of Jesus. When I ran to He who is my refuge and called on His Name, the reach of the enemy was cut short and, the devil could not hold me down. The devil meant it for evil, but God turned it into an opportunity to demonstrate His power. I will admit that in the moment of the attacked, I did have fear, but I realized that I had even more power: power over the enemy himself.

> *Behold, I give unto you power to tread on serpents and scorpions, and over all the power of the enemy: and nothing shall by any means hurt you.*
> *Luke 10:19*

Child of God, we do not have to succumb in fear to the attacks of the enemy. Though being close to God does not except us from adversity, it does keep us from defeat. I can't imagine living in this world and having to face the evil spirits of our day without a close relationship with God.

> *He that dwelleth in the secret place of the most High shall abide under the shadow of the Almighty. I will say of the LORD, He is my refuge and my fortress: my God; in him will I trust. Surely he shall deliver thee from the snare of the fowler, and from the noisome pestilence. He shall cover thee with his feathers, and under his wings shalt thou trust: his truth shall be thy shield and buckler.*

Thou shalt not be afraid for the terror by night; nor for the arrow that flieth by day; Nor for the pestilence that walketh in darkness; nor for the destruction that wasteth at noonday. A thousand shall fall at thy side, and ten thousand at thy right hand; but it shall not come nigh thee.
Psalm 91:1-7

It took me a few days to realize the fullness of what God had done in that Sunday night service. While God was healing others in that service, He was also healing me. My neck and back issue have never been the same since that night. All of the tightness, soreness, pain and problems I had frequently experienced are now gone. That burning sensation that I felt, could it have been healing virtue making right all that was wrong? However it happened, I know this: I have been healed.

I will lift up mine eyes unto the hills, from whence cometh my help.
Psalm 121:1

There in that mountainous region of majestic beauty and wonder, I found a mountain top experience of my own. That Sunday night service will forever be a peak to which I will look back on in awe of God's healing power in my life.

THE CHOICE

In Joshua 14, the children of Judah had come to Joshua at Gilgal to receive their inherited portion of the promised land. Caleb also arrives ready to receive his inheritance. While the others asked

179

for the flat land which would be easiest to settle on, Caleb makes a declaration that lives on through time. He spoke of that glorious by-gone moment in his life when he and Joshua had seen that promised land before they possessed it. The other ten spies were discouraged by the obstacles and thus gave an evil report unto the children of Israel; however, Caleb saw the glory of God's promise. He believed that every enemy and obstacle could be overcome with the help the Lord and pursuing the promised land of God's favor was worth it. Caleb was unwilling to settle for anything less than God's promise and refused to live without the glory; therefore we hear Caleb claim his mountain.

> *Now therefore give me this mountain, whereof the LORD spake in that day; for thou heardest in that day how the Anakims were there, and that the cities were great and fenced: if so be the LORD will be with me, then I shall be able to drive them out, as the LORD said.* Joshua 14:12

How interesting that four hundred years prior to this moment, Abraham had given his nephew, Lot, first choice to that same spot. When he could have had a mountain, Lot chose the fertile plains of Jordan where, without coincidence, he and his family met their doom and destruction. Those well-watered flat plains of Jordan may have seen like a reasonable choice, but the problem is that well watered plains don't quench spiritual thirst for long.

Abraham lived in the land of Canaan while Lot lived among the cities of the plain and pitched his tent toward Sodom. Perhaps, it was just for the view. You know it was attractive, perhaps even glamorous. I picture it to be the Los Angeles of ancient Israel, the Hollywood of the Old Testament! Seemingly glamorous on the outside, but deadly was the sin that lay inside its borders.

But the men of Sodom were wicked and sinners before the LORD exceedingly.
Genesis 13:13

Lot abandoned Canaan, which was that land promised by God, and was lured toward that city of sin called Sodom. Why did he choose the well watered flat lands? Why didn't he want a mountain?

Mountainous land can be dangerous. It takes work, requires patience and it changes how you live and traverse. Lot must have seen that as too much of a sacrifice, too inconvenient for his style; therefore, he picked what looked to be the easiest and most luxurious place to live, absent of so much sacrifice and struggle. To him, the flat land was attractive because of its apparent ease of living. The truth is that, if we try hard enough, we can always find a way to justify our conscience and even attempt to spiritualize our selfish decisions.

Perhaps Lot thought he could make it just fine by his own goodness, being somewhat involved in Sodom's sinful system and still maintain his salvation. He must have thought he was strong enough to fight those spirits on his own. His choice makes apparent his deepest feelings; he didn't need the glory of God that comes from mountaintop moments. That is where Lot deceived himself. We are never strong enough to fight alone. This spiritual fight that we are in can be won only through powerful moments of prayer, wearing the full armor of God and surrendering the battle to the Lord. If we do not have the glory of God in our lives, we are living a life that glorifies only ourselves and our own strength.

It didn't take long before Lot uprooted from the place of his distant view and began living in Sodom. He was now up close and personal with this place of sin and perversion. As wrong as it is, his decision is completely logical. Without mountaintop moments where we encounter God's glory, we have nothing to convict or lead us. There is no standard of righteousness to which we hold ourselves to and evaluate our lives accordingly. It happened then and it happens now, but why? Why do we think we can be involved with the things of the world and still be godly and holy? Why do we try so hard to deceive ourselves into believing that we can have God's unmerited favor and manifold blessing in Canaan, yet persistently inch our way toward the destructive demise of Sodom? The Bible is so clear concerning the distinct decisiveness of our devotion.

> *Love not the world, neither the things that are in the world. If any*
> *man love the world, the love of the father is not in you.*
> *1 John 2:5*

Sin is enmity against God. Compromise always takes us further than we intended to go. It may have seemed justifiable in the beginning but will always, in the end, prove to be inexcusable. Tell me this: how did Lot get to the point that when homosexual men came to his door asking for a man that he tried to give them his daughters? I'll tell you how he got there. He had involved himself in a world of sin and lacked mountaintop moments of prayer and dedication. Without those things and without God, how can a man truly lead his family? The question answers itself, he cannot.

It was only a matter of time before Lot backslid, losing all of his inheritance, wealth, wife and was forced to flee from the city completely. Even after leaving the city behind, his daughters were so indoctrinated by Sodom's wickedness that they seduced their own father. How utterly tragic to see, through Scripture, this family stray so far away from the place of promise that God had made available unto them. Their lives could've been so different, surrounded by the glory of God and guided by His divine purpose. Instead of evil, sin and death, Lot could've left his descendants an inheritance of honor, wealth and prosperity.

God had never issued laws or commandments as an act to show us who is in charge, but rather they were always issued out of His extreme love for us and for our protection. God desires that we prosper and be happily fulfilled in His will.

In contrast to the demise of Lot, we see how Abraham clung solely to God's promises and lived by faith and not sight. I wonder what Abraham's thoughts of Lot were? Perhaps Lot put on quite the front, like so many people do today, so that he would appear to be living a prosperous life amid his compromise. Even if Lot, for a short while, seemed to have a form of godliness, his compromising choice would reveal itself on the surface soon enough. Abraham, whatever his thoughts were of Lot's mistake, was obviously unaffected in his own commitment toward God. Abraham continued to live in the land God had given him possession of, surrounded by blessing and favor. He prospered greatly and is, even to this day, called the father of the faithful. God knew him, loved him and honored him. God had entered into covenant with Abraham, and He takes very seriously the covenants made with His people, as should we take seriously those made with the Lord.

Like Abraham, Caleb also made his decision to possess what God had promised. When the others said that the enemy, the giants, the Anakims are all too great and there would be no way to possess the land, Caleb wholly followed the Lord. If the mountains presents an enemy, "the Lord will be with me, and I will drive them out." Standing in front of Joshua he says with great determination, "Give me this mountain."

Caleb understood that there will always be enemies. No matter where we settle, there will be devils to fight and temptations to conquer. The priority that must drive our devotion is that we live where the glory of God is evident. I can live through a battle and drive out an enemy, but I cannot live without the glory of the Lord. God is calling his people to a place of bold, decisive action where we declared that we will possess the high place that God has made available unto us. If God has set before you a mountain, then don't turn away from the divinely orchestrated experience that awaits you. If you climb to the peak of your promise, there will be unmeasurable glory that surrounds you. I challenge you to let faith motivate your spirit to boldness and claim what God desires for you to possess. If you were Caleb, what would you say?

THE REASON

The Nation Magazine reported, "mountains play a significant role in providing water and food supply to the millions of people in the world. Mountains cover around 22 percent of the surface of the earth."

In essence, we need them. We need them for food and water, without which we cannot live. Although those particular statistics take no claim to spiritual matters, the truth remains: Without spiritual mountaintop moments with God we cannot spiritually live. Those moments are where we find our sustainability and strength to continue on.

In Scripture, Moses is seen on the mountain top numerous times. It was there where he received the ten commandments and saw God's glory. Even in the mountain, Moses denied his flesh and fasted for forty days. When he came down, his countenance glowed with a radiance that can only come from being with God. It doesn't take a scientific study to conclude that a human does not glow with strength and joy after forty days without food or water. That individual would naturally begin to look haggard, sick and malnourished; therefore, there was something on that mountain that gave Moses everything he needed to live. If you can climb your way to a mountaintop with God, your every need will be supplied. You may or may not have earthly resources plenteously flowing through your hand, but you will always be sustained by His power and goodness. God himself will be your bread when you are hungry, your water when you're thirsty and your strength when you are weak. He is, in His fullness, everything we need.

While the faith of some does not struggle to believe in God's ability to show forth his glory, others are afraid of anything they cannot see or control. To them healing sounds incredible and the glory of God sounds life changing, but there are too many dangers and risks. "Why get close to God, anyway?" they ask. "Why climb the mountain when we can stay comfortably at the bottom?

Don't you know there are dangers involved in mountain climbing? You could fall!" says those who have pitched their tent toward Sodom and have set their eyes upon things other than God's promises. They live their lives in fear of what the devil might do to them if they pursue anything more than the miserable flat land of their compromise. "No thanks," they say, "you do what you want, but I'll stay right here at the bottom and play it safe." Friend, you must understand that a mountaintop with Jesus is the safest place one could ever live.

In mountain climbing, the one thing that draws every true climber to the peak is passion. The passionate always posses the prize. The breath-taking sights that await them at the top seem to pull them upward when their weakness wants to turn back. Oh, the countless times Satan has whispered in all of our ears and tried to convince us to turn back or to never climb at all. He strips away our passion for the things of God and leaves us with only fear, a fear that cannot coincide with Godly pursuits yet lays aside its fury at the pursuit of worldly ambition. There so many sit, wallowing miserably at the foot of God's divine promises. How it must please Satan to see so many enslaved at the bottom of the mountain, resigning from all ambitious action to scale the heights of higher ground.

The truth is this: Satan well understands that nothing he has can compare to the glory of God; therefore, he always tries to convince you that the glory isn't worth it. If he can keep us from encountering it then he can deceive you concerning it. But, once we've experienced God's glory, it cannot be denied. Once we come to see the top of the mountain and that His power is real, an unquenchable longing is awakened within us to dwell in His presence.

The reality is that Satan's attacks are not just relegated to the mountain, but he attacks just as much at the bottom. There are just as many, if not more, devils to fight on the plain as there are up toward the peak. They are just perhaps more friendly, seeing that we are not as much of a threat. What a scary place to be! I never want to be so intimidated and manipulated by the enemy that my own satisfaction is gauged by Satan's fury, or lack thereof, against me. So if I will have to face the enemy wherever I dwell, then I'd rather face hell itself with the confidence that God is for me, and victory is waiting at the peak.

The New York Times reported in 1923: "It's been the deadliest mountain climbing season in history, and it's not over. With the tragedies on Mount Rainier in Washington and in Nepal, one question remains: Why do they do it? Why do people regularly risk their lives to summit a mountain peak or scale sheer cliffs?"

"Because it's there," George Mallory famously replied when asked why he was trying to climb Mount Everest—because it's there.

Why do we climb the spiritual mountains of glorious encounter with God? Because the mountain is there! We have not only seen it before us, but we have kept it in our view and set it as our goal. We see the value of the climb and, like Caleb, cannot live unless the summit is attained. I can't live one day unless I know that He is with me. I can't continue on unless I feel His presence surrounding me. I will never survive the onslaught of hell unless His Spirit in within me. I'll never see His glory revealed tomorrow unless I choose to climb today.

How different the tomorrow of Lot's future could have been.

His family could have dwelt in fellowship and covenant with God had Lot not thrown away his opportunity to pursue the glory of God. Even for him, the mountain was there, yet he turned away because he had no desire to climb. So as an escape, Lot decided to replace the view of the mountain with a more enticing view that catered to his fleshly desire. If he didn't have to look at it then he wouldn't feel guilty, so Lot abandoned the mountain completely.

I challenge you to never turn away from the mountain. Until you reach the top, keep it before your eyes. When your heart is being pulled in the direction of compromise, look toward that high place in God. If the mountain is there, you will be reminded of the destiny that awaits you at the top. May we accept the words of Psalm 57:7, "My heart is fixed, O God." My mind is made up!

No where else but on the mountain with Jesus, fellowshipping with Him through deep prayer, will you gain a glimpse of what God has prepared and promised to His people. From that vantage point of power through the Spirit are we allowed to see His kingdom come, His will accomplished and His glory revealed. Dwelling in such closeness and communion with God, Satan's greatest efforts to distract and destroy are defeated by the power of the Name that has saved you.

It is true. I have stood in amazement with uncontrollable tears and watched the glory of God sweep over congregations and take over services. I've seen healing virtue be released through a song of faith or a testimony of God's faithfulness and, in response, I've seen people open up their hearts and truly believe for the first time that God can heal their sick body and broken life. I've seen the gentle, loving Spirit of God break down barriers of hurt and offense, that have torn people apart, and restore relationships. I've seen sinners weep in overwhelming satisfaction while feeling the presence of God for the very first time. I've seen the preached Word of God pull people out of their pews and into an altar, where commitment and consecration are made. I've seen both the high and the humble surrender their hearts and lives to the cause of Christ and His glorious truth. I've seen in my own life just how good and faithful our God is in both the best of times and the worst of times. That is why I say, as Caleb said, "Give me this mountain!"

On the night before he died, the late Dr. Martin Luther King, Jr. eloquently delivered these powerful words in a speech:

"Well, I don't know what will happen now. We've got some difficult days ahead. But it doesn't matter with me now. Because I've been to the mountaintop. And I don't mind. Like anybody, I would like to live a long life. Longevity has its place. But I'm not concerned about that now. I just want to do God's will. And He's allowed me to go up to the mountain. And I've looked over. And I've seen the promised land. I may not get there with you. But I want you to know tonight, that we, as a people, will get to the promised land. And I'm happy, tonight. I'm not worried about anything. I'm not fearing any man. Mine eyes have seen the glory of the coming of the Lord."

So, you want a mountain? Yes, I want a mountain, so! I want a mountain so I can live in victory. I want a mountain so I can be loosed and made free from the curse of sin. I want a mountain so that I can dwell in closeness and covenant relationship with the God of my salvation. I want a mountain so that I can know Jesus and be formed in His likeness. I want a mountain so that I can lead my family in the way of righteousness and holiness. I want a mountain so that I can walk in power and authority over every adversarial force and foe that rises against me. I want a mountain so I can see the promised land and behold the glory of God.

While I continually strive to reach the top, though the journey be hard and long, I make this solemn commitment to the Lord: whatever I face, and until I reach the peak of God's purpose for my life, I'm Still Gonna Praise You.

> *"Lord, you know why you take us through the valleys so low, and you know why you take us through those bitter pains. But while I'm standing here, seeing all my fear, I know I'm going to be all right, Because I'm still gonna serve you, I'm still gonna love you, I'm still gonna praise my way through. So take me through the trials, take me through the pain, because I know whatever comes my way, I'm going to say that, I love you more than I ever have before. I'm still gonna serve you. Still gonna love you. Still gonna praise my way through."*

notes

chapter five

1. YouTube, "Why Chinese Women Spend Fortunes On Plastic Surgery." https://youtu.be/mVpAOr6GYCs

2. Leah Darrow, *The Other Side of Beauty.* Nashville: Thomas Nelson, 2017.

chapter six

1. Clovis Chappell, *Feminine Faces, "The Striking Face,"* *Page 154.* Whitmore & Stone, 1942.

chapter ten

1. *The Nation*, "Importance of Mountains*.*" https://www. google.com/amp/s/nation.com.pk/25-Jan-2018/impor-tance-of-mountains%3fversion=amp.

2. *The Clymb*, "'Because It's There' the Quoteable George Mallory*.*" https://blog.theclymb.com/out-there/be-cause-its-there-the-quotable-george-mallory/

CPSIA information can be obtained
at www.ICGtesting.com
Printed in the USA
LVHW021116130222
710994LV00015B/1308

9 781734 932300